A Time of Change in Hospitality Leadership

A Time of Change in Hospitality Leadership

Chris Sheppardson

BUSINESS EXPERT PRESS

Leader in applied, concise business books

A Time of Change in Hospitality Leadership

Copyright © Business Expert Press, LLC, 2020.

Cover image licensed by Ingram Image, StockPhotoSecrets.com

Cover and interior design by Exeter Premedia Services Private Ltd., Chennai, India

First published in 2020 by
Business Expert Press, LLC
222 East 46th Street, New York, NY 10017
www.businessexpertpress.com

ISBN-13: 978-1-95253-854-4 (paperback)
ISBN-13: 978-1-95253-855-1 (e-book)

Business Expert Press Tourism and Hospitality Management Collection

Collection ISSN: 2375-9623 (print)
Collection ISSN: 2375-9631 (electronic)

First edition: 2020

10 9 8 7 6 5 4 3 2 1

Printed in the United States of America.

Thank you to my two girls—Mimi and Chessie—for the inspiration they give to me each day.

Kipling's *If*, which seems apt to quote when it comes to the topic of leadership.

"IF you can keep your head when all about you
Are losing theirs and blaming it on you,
If you can trust yourself when all men doubt you,
But make allowance for their doubting too;
….Or being lied about, don't deal in lies,
Or being hated, don't give way to hating,
And yet don't look too good, nor talk too wise:
If you can dream—and not make dreams your master;
If you can think—and not make thoughts your aim;
If you can meet with Triumph and Disaster
And treat those two impostors just the same;"

Gioele Camarlinghi, International Hotelier

Abstract

This book is an introduction to the challenge of modern leadership. Leadership has changed from the traditional perspective to be one which is far broader based, with more expected and asked. Leaders today need to consider their stakeholders, their employees, the communities and society in which they operate, the environment, culture and trends. The world has changed so much in the last ten years and many are lagging behind in their understanding. At the same time, we are about to witness a change in generations and the question arises as to whether industry is ready to empower and pass on the baton of leadership?

The main goals are to help students to understand what will asked of them as they become leaders. It is aimed to challenge perceptions, thinking and knowledge. Also, it aims to prepare students to identify how leadership has changed people's lives and help develop critical thinking about the role of leaders in business and in society.

Keywords

chief executive officer (CEO); chief operating officer (COO); chief financial officer (CFO); chief marketing officer (CMO); human resources director (HRD); managing director (MD); millennials; baby boomers; silent generation; Gen Z; artificial intelligence (AI); C-suite; diversity & inclusion (D&I); mergers & acquisitions (M&A); sustainability

Contents

Success is Never Final

"Success is Never Final. Failure is Never Fatal. It's Courage that Counts.(1)"
—**Sir Winston Churchill**

"The years of leadership by the baby boomer generation are moving toward their natural conclusion. It will result in a shift from the one of the most successful business generations ever to that of the millennial's generation: a generation that has been heavily critiqued and is seen to be unproven, untested. Yet there this an exciting prospect as they are progressive and aspiring to see a better world. They have a belief in sustainability in communities, in culture, in business, and environment. Both generations should work together to ease the way, but the chasm between the generations is currently too large. Strangely enough, the differences are not as large as they may appear. The millennials, in truth, are only a reflection of the baby boomers who have heavily influenced them. Both generations began their journeys with strong ideals. The baby boomers compromised in line with the challenges that they faced, but still raised another generation stressing the ideals that they still held close to them, so a bridge should be able to be built. How can this be achieved?" —**by Chris Sheppardson, Edited by Lauran Bush MA, Research support by Iwona Drozdz, 2020**

Acknowledgements

It is only correct that I acknowledge a number of their support, guidance and friendship during the writing of this book including:

- Abigail Tan, CEO, St.Giles Hotel Group
- Adam Elliott, Co-Founder, Paragon Hospitality
- Michael Gray, former VP for London with Hyatt
- Ken McCulloch, MUH Hotels
- Bob Cotton OBE
- Gioele Camarlinghi, hotelier
- Marco Truffelli, hotelier
- David Coubrough, Chair, Royal Academy of Culinary Arts
- Nick Metcalfe, Chess Partnership
- Russell Kett, Chairman, London Office, HVS
- Ramesh Vala OBE, Global Ambassador, Ince
- Kevin Watson, Managing Director, Amadeus
- Frank Bothwell, Founder, Thomas Franks
- Alex Buchanan, Founder, Catering Scotland
- Karen Friebe, Partner, Bird & Bird
- David Read, Chairman, Prestige Purchasing
- Doug Tetley, MD Europe, Delaware North
- Hamish Cook, Executive Director, En-Route International
- Gavin Brooking. Hotel Advisor and consultant
- Donald Sloan, Chair, Oxford Cultural Collective
- Kathryn Pretzel Shiels, Consultant
- Marianna Alfa, Founder, Blossom Hospitality
- John Harris, Co-founder, Confab
- Vicky La Trobe, Consultant

Thank you to all the above and to all those interviewed during the process from all across the world.
Our thanks.

Introduction

The Time for New Leadership in Hospitality

"The most dangerous leadership myth is that leaders are born—that there is a genetic factor to leadership. That's nonsense; in fact, the opposite is true. Leaders are made rather than born (3)." —**Warren Bennis**

There are many who argue that leaders are born, that leaders will possess the natural attributes to be destined for the role. It is true that there are those who are very naturally suited to leadership, and in a simpler age, this ethos had more truth in it. It is an old-fashioned perspective and has less substance for today's world. Everyone has a view upon leadership, but very few understand it.

Leadership today is not as simple as being solely about character. The world is evolving at such pace that leaders need to be prepared to live in a world which will constantly be uncertain and that will be almost consistently vulnerable. Some will argue that 9/11 changed the world. Others that the artificial intelligence (AI) revolution and the globalization attached changed traditional models and approaches. The pace of change that has been generated has certainly created new possibilities. Many will argue that the demands of shareholders have seemed to be ever-more demanding and have placed increased pressures upon leadership teams.

Society too has changed, and the emerging generations have grown up in arguably the safest ever environment, which has naturally meant that they too will think differently to previous generations. In previous eras, making a good living was the primary objective. The old saying that "mortgages make mice of men" existed for good reason. Many talk today about the fear of failure, but in previous generations, one expected to compromise on one's aspirations and hopes. Past generations were focused on lower expectations. One leading Industry CEO started his career as a chef so as to escape the fate of his brothers in going down the old coal mines. He was driven by a desire to build a life as far away from having to face that choice and today, having been a very successful leader, he sees his wealth as the basis for his children to have security and choice; to never have to face the choices he had to make. This is not an isolated example. The greatest success of the baby boomer generation has lain in building wealth and safe environments for their children to have the freedom to aspire for greater. The irony, of course, is that this has also created the fault lines and tensions that many have struggled to understand.

Today's generations are more ambitious and free in their aspirations. This has had its own consequences as real economics create their own barriers, but the social change, which has taken place over the last 20 years, needs recognizing. Many of today's problems have been thirty years in the making. One can argue that a safe world and strong economies have allowed poor behaviours to thrive. The traditional pillars, on which many companies were founded, have been eroded as leaders focused on a combined focus of increased profit and reduced investment in the core pillars. Many of the problems that business face today have become an inevitability of that dual focus.

All the preceding arguments have a level of merit and all have impacted to create a complex landscape for leaders to navigate.

The millennial generation has come to force as the largest group in employment today. They have often felt disappointed in the last decade by the leadership they have experienced, and they have a desire for better. They are the most educated, diverse, and inclusive generation to emerge yet, and they are naturally making the arguing for greater change. They have strong ideals, and they are coming into positions of influence. This should lead to a far more progressive agenda emerging.

The baby boomer generation, in contrast, has been one of the finest business generations ever. They have faced a lot of criticism in how they have struggled to nurture the millennials through. Some of this has been fair; some not so. The irony is the millennials are a reflection of the baby boomers and the previous generation, the so called Silent Generation, just their more personal ideology. The millennials want to live without the compromises made by their parents. In their mind, that was their choice and they view a different way forward.

The millennials have been brought up on strong ideals by their parents. The baby boomers started themselves with strong idealism, and they have broken many barriers. They have parented with greater levels of love, care, and education in what matters. They have laid the land for change. It will be the next generations that will see this change through.

The world faces some serious problems. Many countries run a danger of two societies almost running alongside one another in parallel. Diversity & Inclusion is still a major concern as is the environmental and social sustainablity. It will need a genuine philosophy of change to create the momentum needed. The signs are that this is building, and it could well be that we stand at the start of a new golden era that will require a new style of leadership. This is the essence of the text to follow.

Today's leaders need to be prepared to listen and learn like never before; they need to be able to adapt; be open to other's ideas, for they will not be able to understand all that is going on around them; and be able to be leaders that their teams can relate to. No longer can leaders be aloof, or inaccessible. They need to be genuine, authentic, and visible. One of the most common words being used at this time is "trust." There has been a general erosion of trust in leaders, in institutions, and in business. Now, as we face life post Covid-19, leaders need to fast rebuild the lost trust with their teams and customers. How can this be done? It will require a change in behaviors and mindset.

Leadership is anything but the black and white subject that so many seem to believe when they write on the subject. Part of the motivation for writing the following text is that too often, experts write on the subject as though it can be learned through the management theory, and that leadership can be easily classified. Maybe, to a level, this was once true, but no more. At the same time, the millennial generation is coming to their time to lead and leadership is changing in nature just as this time comes. The following book aims to explain many of the frictions and tensions that exist in this evolution and outline the challenges to be faced.

Leadership today is very much about a combination of learning, listening, and adapting as one develops along with being able to unite people in a common goal. It has never been a simple task, and most experienced leaders will admit that they have experienced failure as well as success. The two often run hand-in-hand with one another. If one aspires to leadership, then it is important to understand this simple fact. You will need to accept failure and be able to learn from it. From failure will come success.

It was Kipling who very correctly wrote:
"If you can meet with Triumph and Disaster
And treat those two impostors just the same" (2).

Leadership is a test of character, but it is often the learnings one finds in failure and from others that allow leaders to work beyond both triumph and disaster; to understand what is real and what is false, what matters, and who can make a difference.

One will often find the most experienced and able leaders talking about the scars they carry, as it is a test that challenges every part of a person's character. It was Tony Blair, the former British Prime Minister, who noted that his unpopularity grew in the direct opposite direction to the more competent he became as a leader. Leadership is not always a logical journey. Success and failure are regular companions as the importance of leadership plays a central role in all our lives.

Leadership has long sat at the heart of most cultures. As the pace of change is so fast today, it is important to share knowledge and ideas in a far more proactive fashion than has been needed to be the case before. As the world has become more open, more transparent, so leadership has had to change in many ways. It has been on its own journey during the digital age. It has not always been an easy journey, as many have taken the advancements of the new age and not always fully understood its ramifications. There has been a growing cry for a stronger balance to be found in business between wealth creation, talent, and sustainability. This is a time for a reset in order to solve the problems that do exist and to build stronger structures. It is a time which is asking for new ideas, thinking and increased social compassion.

Photo Abigail Tan CEO, St.Giles Group of Hotels

Abigail Tan, Chief Executive of the St. Giles Group of Hotels, which runs hotels in New York, London, Europe, and Malaysia, and who is viewed to be an emerging leadership voice, noted in an interview for this book that:

> Some of the reasons for change (In leadership) I believe is the entrance in the general workforce and leadership roles of Xennials and Millenials. Natives of a more interconnected world, both generations respond to a collaborative, shared leadership style, where input from all team members, regardless of "role" is not just welcomed, but actively encouraged. Another reason for change is the pace of society—our world moves at a digital speed and knowledge is ever evolving; therefore, decision making has been decentralized to adapt to the need for quick informed actions.
>
> The role of leadership has evolved from having a dominant figure who enforces rule and power, top down, to a leader who delegates and empowers to create other leaders within the organisation. Structures have gone from a sharp hierarchy triangle, to one that looks wider and flatter.
>
> Leaders today create the vision, and set the direction, while motivating and engaging the team to deliver that vision. This has become a more inclusive and collaborative process rather than exclusive.

In a world that is ever more closely connected and transparent, strangely, many feel more vulnerable and less safe. Leadership is having to evolve and change to combat this growing insecurity and fear. It is finding its way in the new digital age and has made a few wrong turns along the road. It is being questioned to a level not seen before.

Many argue that, with the 24/7 nature of social media and mainstream media, the traditional pillars of society have been eroded, as those pillars were simply not prepared for the scrutiny that came with advancement. Respect has declined alongside. As the world became more open, the bar has risen in what has been expected of a leader, and very simply, many have struggled to raise their game. It is not all their fault. Pressures too have increased, but many leaders of the past were not always the great figures of stature that are sometimes portrayed. Leaders have become concerned about how their own natural weaknesses may be portrayed and withdrew a step, creating a chasm between leadership and many teams. It has taken time to learn that most are very forgiving of those weaknesses and can often relate with something not so far removed from the real world: a fact that Boris Johnson found during the UK General Election of 2019 when his popularity almost grew within the more sustained attacks on his character. It did show a gulf between the media and the person on the street.

It is certainly true that many media reporters have moved from being commentators on events to being opinion leaders, as this attracts increased levels of listener, and therefore, impacts on the commercial performance of a media outlet. Media outlets have encouraged their journalists to develop a voice of their own, which does fly in the face of the job of reporting on the facts. Opinion has become more important than objectivity. Is it right that a journalist with very little experience in leadership has the power to influence public opinion against someone who does carry the burden of responsibility?

It is interesting that during COVID-19, many have turned away from some of the leading journalists, as trust in their motives have become questioned.

Of course, leaders need to possess many admirable personal characteristics, but leadership, quite rightly, is a deeper topic than merely behavior. It is how leaders are able to bring people together, how they are able to build trust, and how they are able to gain knowledge in order to be able to make accurate decisions.

There has been a major debate quietly taking place in the background, as many do feel that the baby boomer generation has failed in the way, in that it has not nurtured and developed the millennials and Generation Z as they themselves were once nurtured. There is a rising voice for a less self-interested approach to business and a greater focus on building sustainable business for the long term.

Whether this is a fair accusation or not will be debated in the pages to follow. It is certainly fair to argue that the average age of leaders has increased, and there does appear to have been a growing distrust of empowering and more importantly, enabling the young. The average age of chief executive officers (CEOs) has increased in recent years, and the

U.S. Presidential Election of 2020 will be fought by two men in their 70s. There is no evidence that age and experience result in a better leader. Arguably, the finest presidents have been younger than most CEOs today when they came to power. Consider Lincoln, Clinton, Obama, and JFK. Leadership is not just about sound judgment that can come from experience, but also about inspiring others and setting out a vision that others will follow.

There is an argument that the baby boomer generation has remained in power for too long, made the most wealth in history, and has proven to have been a barrier for young talent breaking through.

Of course, the issue is more complex because companies have become more streamlined in recent years and have had to rebuild from the fallout from the 2008/2009 Great Crash. As a result, many younger talents have not had the opportunity to be able to gain the skills of previous generations and naturally have gaps in their knowledge. It creates a cycle whereby the baby boomer generation still to this day possesses a stronger all-round knowledge and skill set, and the overall problem intensifies. It is a problem that can be solved. Abigail Tan commented that:

> This gap has emerged because we have a multi-generational workforce at the same time when our world is experiencing a fast-paced cultural evolution," commented Abigail Tan in the interview for this book. "On one hand, you have young Matures and Baby Boomers seeing a world that they helped create undergo an almost complete transformation. On the other hand, we have the millennial generation who are natives to this fast-paced cultural shift. Therefore, it may seem that these generations have a clash in values and expectations, but like most things, when we delve further, we see there are fewer differences than what's perceived. When the gap is bridged or the perspective shifts, we tend to see transformation leadership.
>
> With regards to the fewer emergence of talent in senior roles compared to twenty or thirty years ago, this may be a result of companies streamlining responsibilities, therefore there are fewer roles and of course, the talent pool is larger given our multi-generation workforce.

Abigail Tan's comments are very apt as once we strip everything back; the differences between generations are not as great as they may appear, but the challenge that we face today is to ensure that once again, the emerging generations are nurtured effectively, and that a marriage between the generations can be found. Both can learn from one another, and as Abigail Tan notes, if we can build the bridge, then this will lead to dynamic change.

The role of leadership is posing new questions to all. In hospitality, there are many new challenges that have emerged from how the role of asset managers, shareholders, and venture capitalists have impacted increasingly in the last 20 years to how the customer's expectations have changed; employees too.

The following is based on over 100 interviews and discussions with leading hospitality figures from all across the world during the opening months of 2020. We would like to thank all those that gave up their time to give us their thoughts, insights, and opinions.

The aim is to be thought provoking, ask questions of you (the reader) to reflect upon and represent the views, not of scholars, but of real leaders from the hospitality industry. There may be much that you do not agree with in the following and also much that you do. The aim is to challenge your own understanding of leadership and provide an insight into how many leaders view the industry and its challenges.

One of the prevailing arguments of many leaders today is that the knowledge base of many of those emerging is not as strong as it once was. The argument is that many younger talents are naturally brighter and even more educated, but the overall knowledge of business and people has fallen. Whether this is right or wrong will be debated in the pages to follow, but regardless, it is important to help challenge the thinking of each reader, to help challenge and develop each reader's own understanding and confidence in how they view leadership.

The need to develop strong leaders is as central an issue today as it ever has been, maybe even of more importance. We will argue that often business in recent years has failed talent, and we ask what more needs to be done—would what you do to create change?

Has the business environment changed so much in recent years that infrastructures are struggling to meet that change and are less effective?

Is the overall structure of the industry good enough to support the long-term development of talent? Is it progressive in its thinking? Is it inclusive?

Can industry leaders today play a bigger role in society and really make a stand for hospitality? Are the hotel schools aligned with industry and preparing talent ready for the workplace?

These are all major questions that need to be asked and answered. There is a desire and a need for some new thinking when it comes to leadership in hospitality. It is a world-class industry, but one that will constantly evolve in line with changing fashions, customer demands, and social tastes. It is an industry that attracts some exceptional talent across many disciplines from leadership to culinary, and it has the ability to become an even more important global industrial sector. To achieve all this, it needs to ensure that it can develop, attract, and importantly, retain the best talent to lead the way into that future.

It is not a simple mission, but it is a worthy one.

The following text will explore all the key questions and aim to ask new questions for consideration. It also includes live case studies and examples of leaders who are not just the normal high-profile figures that one will often read about but also genuine, real leaders drawn from industry, of all ages and differing backgrounds, who bring a different aspect of leadership to be considered.

However, a positive story to finish the Introduction; one that does illustrate the care of leadership for others. During the COVID-19 crisis, there was one story to emerge that highlighted this. A senior industry player spoke of his pain in having to make many redundancies. His message to those he cut was "We do care about you. We want to work with you again and we will work hard now so that we can meet again."

Afterward, he talked to EP Insights about his reasoning:

I was, I am frustrated with how industry leaders have said so little about our people during this crisis. We need to show compassion, so I felt it was right to be upfront and tell them early what the truth is. They knew the truth and the feedback that I have had is that they have respected the way we have gone about it. We have said that in any new job opening, one of those being redundant will have preference if they want to re-join. We are a family. It is my duty to them that we will work as hard as we can so that we can re-employ as many as we can, as soon as we can.

Why am I frustrated by others? Our people deserve to be treated with respect and with compassion. They are waiting on us, on our actions and it must be a tough place to be. I have prided myself throughout my life that I have relied only on me . . . but this crisis would have taken that away from me and I would have had no option but to rely on others. Horrible place to be.

My hope is that as an industry we do see real compassion and care for those that lose their jobs. I know the estimates are beyond 300,000, maybe 400,000 (in the UK) and we need to stand together—those who have lost their jobs and employers who can, in time, re-employ them.

"I absolutely believe this is the right message for this time and the right way that we should behave" (4).

At the end of the day, all leaders are judged by their tenure. How people feel safe, economically prosperous, motivated, inspired, cared for—it is the challenge for all leaders. Reputations are made and lost by how a leader can bring all this together. It can be fickle, often pressurized, but few leaders would miss out on the opportunity to lead.

Joyce and Raissa de Haas, Founders of Double Dutch
An Opening Thought

The reality of leadership is that it is very different to what you have been taught. In practice, it is almost the polar opposite. I have had a few amazing leaders in my career who saw my potential and were not frightened to invest in me. After that, I went through a series of leaders who worked with fear, with financial targets in mind, with no training, no development. It was then that I discovered that was the culture of the company I was working with. It was then my purpose to create a momentum for change.

I have a belief that those that work in Hospitality do care about others. About protecting each other, come from similar values and they are the ones that can make a difference.

(Victoria La Trobe, Industry Consultant)

PART I

Leadership at the Heart of Business

CHAPTER 1

Why Is Leadership of Such Importance?

All across the world, cultures have long revered its leaders. The reason for this probably stems from somewhere deep within its tribal heritage, when leaders played such a pivotal role in society and business. Think "memorable leader" and one's mind will likely be drawn to characters such as Winston Churchill, JFK, Martin Luther King, George Washington, Abraham Lincoln, Margaret Thatcher, Barrack Obama or many of our greatest sporting idols: Bobby Moore, Pele, Maradona, Megan Rapinoe, Francois Pienaar, Tom Brady, Joe Namath, and Richie McCaw, who all became cult heroes and inspired children all around the world to seek to emulate their achievements.

All were exceptional in their discipline; Churchill arguably one of the very most so, as he was also a talented writer, historian, orator, and artist, let alone how he inspired a nation with their backs against the wall. Maybe there is something in his diversity of skills that went beyond what was needed and simply expected, because leadership today is consistently being asked to "be more." Of course, this is a contradiction as it is unlikely, with Churchill's known weaknesses, that he would have come close to a position of power today. Neither JFK nor Bill Clinton. The bar today has been raised in some ways, and yet lowered in others. More is asked and yet human weakness is less forgiven. In many ways, leadership became too "Alpha" during the most recent era. Many leaders felt unable to show vulnerability and yet it is often weakness and failure though which teaches empathy and humility.

The "Alpha" factor is discussed and analyzed later in the book as it is not followers who are not forgiving of weakness and vulnerability; in fact, it helps create bonds. No, it has been leaders and shareholders who have been fast to see weakness as a problem. The result is that often the wrong characters have become leaders rather than those with real empathy, emotional intelligence, strong value set and understanding of communities and culture. It is for good reason that trust has been so eroded. It does not just happen by accident. It is the result of a major fault line.

There are numerous contradictions when it comes to the topic of "leadership" as leadership is often about a moment in time when one person brings a group together in pursuit of a common goal. The leader is the glue and the inspiration to achieve something which is beyond the norm. Hence why it is often easier to admire the sports captain than the business or political leader as it is a far simpler landscape to navigate and understand. Sport is as black and white as winning or losing. Business leadership today includes overseeing a large variety of topics from business performance to diversity to sustainability (economic, cultural, social, and environmental) to managing the customer experience to talent development.

Just as life is not as clear cut as black or white so it is with the topic of leadership. There are many leaders who have been an inspiration for a short period of time; others who only became leaders when a moment in time arrived, which brought the best out of them. The heart of leadership lies in character and it is often developed over time. One could compare leadership to a fine wine—it improves and matures with age, if nurtured well, but all can be lost with a simple mistake. However, this is only part of the overall picture.

Understanding the heart and essence of leadership is part of the learning. Maybe one of the best examples has been the learning that most have to do in the field of diversity and inclusion. It has taken a long time to break down barriers and to educate a broader, more progressive approach which has delivered strong results. This area alone has not been an easy journey, but one which has been important as many teams today are multicultural as well as being multi-disciplined and skilled. That is the essence of hospitality: a meritocracy and home for all.

Strong managers are often confused with leaders and yet the two skill sets are very much separate. Management is about detail and organization. Leadership is about seeing something which others cannot see and then leading a team to achieve an objective.

Marc Verstringhe, the founder of Catering & Allied, a leading Food Service management company in London during the 1980s and 90s, described his role as a leader in two ways.

His first description was "I stand at the top of the mountain and am able to gaze across the whole valley below. My management team stand halfway up the mountain and as such their gaze will be naturally impeded. One cannot expect them to see what I can see from my position."

His second was "I have three Managing Directors and all three will rarely, if ever be performing well at the same time. My job is to stand with the one who is struggling at that time and give them the support they need. Then I move to the next as they get back to speed."

Marc is a unique man whose formative years were spent in the war-torn country of Belgium during the Second World War. It taught him to have a strong empathy for people and communities plus a love for the fine things in life. His passion was food and wine. Many followed the vision that he set out as it resonated: a belief that a love of great food that would bring people together and lighten up the day. It spoke a positive message that said that there is more to life than just work. For Marc, life was not about management science but about believing in something bigger, which all could aspire to and believe in. This, in turn, inspired his teams.

Many of Marc's generation grew up in an era which did have a different perspective, a respect for human life and careers. As they grew up in some of the toughest times, they understood how work and their leadership impacted on the self-respect and psychology of those under their charges. They also understood the importance of understanding human failings and the need to have fun. Gardner Merchant, a former global Food Service company in the 70s, 80s, and 90s, tried to have a philosophy of never dismissing anyone. They believed that security of tenure would make their people feel safe and therefore enabled to take risk. If they did fail, they would be quietly moved to another role. It was a different era but, just as today, they understood that it was when a person feels safe that they feel trusted enough to take risk.

This does highlight one of the strange questions to consider. Employees generally prefer not to take any risk which may place them in any chance of being seen to fail. Many leaders talk about their people having the courage to take initiative and yet it is very hard to achieve. A former leading UK CEO used to remark: "Why is it that no one comes to me with a solution, only with problems to solve?" The higher education system is designed to nurture talent to think for themselves, to problem solve, to act with an independent mind: so why does this not transfer into actions within the work environment?

There are many leaders today who worked under those from that period of the 80s and 90s and who will privately remark of the fun that they had in their early days. They will acknowledge the leeway and the time they were given to grow as professionals. It was as the old saying goes, a simpler time when communications were far less developed and mistakes could be easily hidden, or be left unseen. More time and privacy naturally created understanding. The advancement in communication, in both speed and transparency has created greater pressure on all.

One result is that often those same leaders, who developed in an era with greater understanding of their mistakes, will be far more demanding on today's emerging talent. It is not so much that they have forgotten the behaviors and lessons from the past but that they are under more personal pressure, there is more scrutiny, businesses are under more pressure and shareholders are constantly seeking greater returns. A balance has arguably been lost which many want to find again. It is less about a desire for shareholders not to receive great returns but a desire that companies do have strong values once again, that leaders can be more accessible, able to lead with freedom and that talent can flourish. There is good reason why the leading newspaper of London's financial and business sector, *The Financial Times*, began a campaign in late 2019 titled "Capitalism Reset."

Leadership is not about a personal agenda or one's own interests but about something bigger than a single person. It is about representing and bringing the best out of a group, a team, a community. There are many CEOs who are not good leaders but are portrayed as such. There are often better leaders hidden in the shadows and this is why there are so many contradictions that need to be worked through and understood. Leadership has never been a popularity contest and it was the great Mark Twain who commented that "Whenever one is on the side of the majority, it is time to pause and reflect" (4a). However, in recent times, populism has grown in strength and has actually created it's own strength. It is becoming harder for leaders to take center ground positions and oppose both populism and extremism. However, to do so simply comes with the territory for those who are leaders.

Act Bigger and Think Bigger

It was JFK who, in 1961, spoke the famous words "Ask not what your country can do for you but what you can do for your country" (5). Sixty years on and this is remarkably still the same ethos that sets the benchmark for leadership today. In today's world, leaders must excel in their work but also contribute to society; they must act bigger and think bigger than themselves and the immediate.

At the time of writing, the world is facing the Coronavirus and this ethos is even more at the forefront. We are all being asked to think bigger and more broadly again, for our communities, for the vulnerable and for each other. Many have found this period has been a period of resetting in values, objectives, and priorities. Many argue that this reset has long been needed.

A few of the growing concerns of work environments is that thinking has become far narrower due to the longer hours that many today work, having less time to reflect, with the increased levels of information available and the increased pressure on margins. There is a strong argument that certain skill sets, especially networking and social competencies, have declined. There is also a belief that younger emerging talent are arguably more intelligent but perhaps not as worldly wise and empathetic to the world-at-large. In a world which has become increasingly transparent, leaders are expected to have almost spotless records and few, if any, skeletons in their past. Yet at the same time, there has never been less trust in leadership. How can this be the case?

One of the issues which is often not written about enough is just how many lost trust after 2008–2009 with leaders and with business. One challenge of today is that many do not aspire to be leaders as once was the case. The emerging generations, both Millennials and Gen Z, are better educated than any previous generation and see less barriers to upward social mobility, in gender and in race. They have arguably been the generation which has been most affected by the fall out in 2008–2009 and now with the Coronavirus. They have faced adversity and they do possess the energy to see real change take place. They also believe in the importance of communities to a greater extent than the baby boom generation. Interestingly, they have been quiet and respectful, waiting for their moment to be able to create change.

They have lost faith in leadership from the top and instead opted to find leadership which is more local and more personal. This can help explain the #MeToo campaign which was, in many ways, a rebellion against the behaviors of the old school. It also helps to explain why the "Black Lives Matter" campaign took off with such energy and gathered such momentum during 2020.

When did this Change take place?

Everyone has a different moment that they can point to. In the UK, many will point toward the start of the Blair Government (1997–2000) when so many held a firm belief that Blair would create a genuine momentum of change; that politics would change. When it became clear that this would not happen, so a disillusionment set in which then came to the fore with the fallout from the Iraq War.

In the United States, one can argue that the 2000 Election left a feeling of disillusionment and of course, the Iraq War confirmed this to many. The Obama presidency promised much but still the much hoped for change did not quite manifest itself.

It is no coincidence that the genuine movements of the last few years have had no clear leader: #MeToo, The Extinction Rebellions, even Black Lives Matter. The cause is championed but there appears to be no figurehead as was the case in the days of Martin Luther King or with the great CND marches in London at the start of the 1980s. Does this illustrate the desire to be part of a community rather than the need to lead? Does it illustrate the desire for social change but with a difference?

Suddenly what matters is not leadership but real social issues which do impact on daily life. It was one of the contradictions of the emerging generations in that they hold a global view but also a very local one. They want their communities to feel strong, their schools, their hospitals but it is less about the nation as a whole as they have lost trust in leaders.

They are also more forgiving and want to be led by those who are genuine and authentic so they can find that elusive trust once again. Maybe many people find trust in those that have weaknesses and are human? Maybe those who have failed have learnings that can make them better leaders? Was the world a safer place under Bill Clinton or George W Bush? How was it that Churchill could achieve something that was clearly beyond his very able predecessor, Neville Chamberlain (6)?

Why is it that George W Bush has been seen as more friendly, accessible, considered, genuine and almost statesmanlike post being president than Bill Clinton?

Character is not the result of navigating life's challenges safely but often through failure. As Churchill once famously remarked "Success is going from failure to failure without losing your enthusiasm" (7), although it has been rumored that Abraham Lincoln too said these words.

One of the challenges today is asking aspiring leaders to be unafraid to fail so that they can be better; to think more deeply and passionately about major issues and to have principles that they are willing to take an active stand for. There is no doubting their passion for environmental and global issues, but can they be leaders?

The ethos is simple. Leadership cannot be taught just by textbooks; it needs to be nurtured and developed through exposure to the world beyond work and home. Potential leaders need to be prepared to fail in order to succeed. One needs to feel something deep to be able to lead. This can be pain; it can be passion. Leadership comes from having a desire and motivation to create change, to stand for something which is bigger than just oneself.

It has been a major concern in recent decades, almost since the dawn of digitalization back in the 1980s, that many leaders became one dimensional, focused only on financial results, on wealth and not enough on people, communities and that leaders had placed genuine and authentic principles to one side and focused more on "what is in it for me?"

Worse still is that many neither trust their leaders nor feel safe enough to be able to express themselves or to take risk.

This is not leadership as defined by what many are seeking. There is little doubt that the 2008–2009 crash has played a major role in building the chasm between leadership, teams and in eroding trust. It will be interesting to review how historians write about the years 2008–2020 and how kind they will be to those in leadership roles.

When the financial crash of 2008–2009 took place, many noted at the time that it would be a time to learn key lessons; that leaders would need to learn from the errors made. At the time, it was described as a major heart attack to the system which would create the basis for necessary correction as behaviors had changed with the long period of prosperity.

It was the financial sectors which took the brunt of the criticism. Business faced a turbulent period with the "age of austerity" being announced but the question remains, were any business or leadership lessons from the 2008–2009 crash learnt? Did the values of those in leadership positions change and adapt in response to the crisis?

Arguably, behaviors actually declined further. Many directors protected themselves during the fallout and it was the lower and middle income levels that faced the worst. Lost employees were replaced by automated systems, business processes and the gap between the wealth of senior players and those in middle management actually got greater. Research shows that the remuneration of senior players during this period of time doubled whilst the remuneration of middle management only grew by between 25 and 30 percent over the same period. The argument was that senior players were being rewarded via greater bonuses on business results and returns to the shareholder. A fair argument even if one dimensional. It would naturally lead to increased self-interest and one dimensional thinking which focused almost solely on results. Even if this was understandable to rebuild from the crash, it was clearly not a long-term, sustainable approach.

Many leaders have spoken with genuine surprise in recent years over some of the statistics to emerge about the disengagement of employees and the erosion in trust in leadership teams. It is surely a natural evolution from the above? It is also natural that today there is a genuine call for better leadership, broader vision and a focus on building a business strategy that embraces both environmental and social sustainability.

Back in 2008–2009, many believed major errors had been made, that values had eroded and that a new narrative would come to the fore alongside most companies making a major correction to their approaches. However, in truth, this did not happen.

One of the leading perspectives, following the crash, was that it was those in middle and lower income brackets who took the brunt of the fallout and that very few directors were affected. The change in those at board level during this period was only at 1 percent higher than what was the norm each year yet both the UK and the United States faced high numbers of job losses.

Were lessons learnt? It certainly changed much in financial services with greater regulation and stricter policies. One would like to think that the narrative did change in business and society too but little really changed as it should have done. However, the counter is that it has laid the ground for change to come now as the emerging generations do see a different perspective and landscape.

Hospitality has arguably suffered from the impact of this change with less visible leaders, less accessible leadership and an erosion of investment in people. There are many that yearn for more visible leadership again, hoteliers walking the floor and being with their guests, leaders taking platforms to talk to their people and hospitality ultimately playing a real role in society again.

And here lies the core challenge and underlines why leadership is so important today. Hospitality is all about caring for others. It is about an act of service. It is also about celebrating togetherness through great food, wine, experiences, and people. It has arguably a genuine opportunity to play a bigger social role than ever.

If one goes back forty or fifty years, local communities were led by the local priest, the local doctor, the family lawyer, the bank manager, and the hospitality manager lagging slightly behind. Since that time, bank managers have been centralized and no longer play a key social role. The doctor has withdrawn, as has the lawyer. The church has been eroded by scandal and change. The irony, of course, is that millennials do want to see a far greater focus on local communities. The pendulum is swinging back.

The one person left standing is the hospitality manager. Hospitality is a combination at core of care, people, and togetherness, an ethos which does make it stand tall and apart. There is a strong argument that cultural and social sustainability will become ever more important in the years post Covid-19. Hotels and restaurants can represent their communities; create a voice that does tell the story of the local culture and community to a far greater extent than has been the case. Hotels and restaurants can stand tall for their communities.

This is why leadership is so important today. It has both a social and a business role to play. It stands for something that is genuinely important in all our psyches.

This particularly was well illustrated during the Coronavirus lockdown when many in Hospitality did not stand idly by but volunteered to support many charitable and social initiatives. Many Food Service companies turned their kitchens into operations to prepare and deliver food to the vulnerable. Large exhibition centers and hotels became hospitals. They did whatever they could, for no reward or income; they did it, volunteered their time and took great pride in doing so because it was and is, very simply, in their DNA. It did illustrate just how the Industry can stand and make a difference socially as well as a business.

In May 2020, a group of leading chefs in the UK came together to create a new association, named the Ethical Chefs Association (ECA). They released a statement which noted:

> Born from a desire to help tackle the ever-more pressing issue of food poverty in the UK, The Ethical Chefs Association is being formed by a group of hospitality industry chefs who are coming together to raise awareness of the extent of food poverty in the UK and to unite supporters to help alleviate suffering caused by food poverty.
>
> There is genuine trust in chefs who have a passion for food and for service. There is a growing desire for Industry collaboration which this would represent. There are many who see an opportunity for genuine social change to be led by a group of great chefs from across the country who want to make a difference. This is about culinary professionals who are normally in competition, placing aside those differences, and working together toward a big picture agenda and creating necessary and positive change.
>
> This is not just another Industry body but an alliance of leading chefs who want to create an agenda for change. Food is arguably the one universal language that reaches all. It can be food, therefore, that can serve to bring people together and create a level of social change that many desire and want.

As The Guardian reported, there are over 5 million families in food poverty the UK, a situation which has been exacerbated by measures to combat COVID-19. The ECA will work to a two-pronged approach: to lobby companies within the hospitality industry to provide support and for individual members to offer their services and chefs to support local food projects, food banks, family centres, meal distribution operations and reduce the number of families affected by hunger and lack of food.

This is not about placing any company's agenda at the forefront but ensuring that through food, the industry can help support the vulnerable in society and change lives.

Last weekend witnessed the VE Anniversary celebrations. 75 years since the end of the Second World War. It seems very apt, therefore, to launch at this time after we have faced a crisis that many have described as this generation's war. 1945-50 saw real social change with the founding of the NHS. Wouldn't be good if this was the start of a movement for chefs coming together to combat poverty? (8)

It was quite a statement. In short, it said that they did not believe that leaders would be able to collaborate well enough as they placed their own interests before a common goal. They believed that companies were simply too competitive with each other and that more could be gained through collaboration. The success of this venture is still to be seen but this does not detract from the power of the statement. Many want to see leaders begin to think bigger and act with greater social compassion.

The Opportunity

One of the genuine opportunities that the Hospitality Industry possesses is how to be the center point of communities and be able to play a major social role. Hospitality does have a role to play in bringing these communities together again post Coronavirus. This is a role that it can play which is ongoing.

We pride ourselves on how we bring people together and then we talk in big terms about the importance of our brand. It is all about people and it should be. Business has evolved in many ways, often in good ways, but we should not forget the founding pillar of Hospitality, to bring people together and to care for them. If we forget about our communities we serve, then it will be our loss. I believe that hotels take a lot from our communities so we should become a part of the community. It could be for charity, sitting on local committees, inviting people to local meetings, giving them a glass of wine, becoming their friend. It is a very exciting part of being a leader, to lead your people in supporting communities.

(Michael Gray, Former Regional VP for Hyatt in London)
It is a view which is supported by others:

There is no question over this. We have to influence, support communities and schools. The service has to be adapted so that it is part of the community. It is a real opportunity and will need some new thinking.

(Marc Dardenne, CEO, Luxury Brands Europe—Accor)

It is not just hotels: I believe we all have a responsibility to give back to our communities and to be conscious of the impact we are making on society. Hotels are such a critical part of any community—they are a microcosm of the local culture; they are often a large employer within the local community, they are a major economic driver for that community. As such hotels have a responsibility to give back and improve communities in which they call home.

(Martin Rinck, EVP and Chief Brand Officer at Hilton in Vancouver)

I have no doubt that hotels play a key social role in the world and more in local environments. It is essential to increase our focus on how we aid our local community as well as our impact on the environment

(Ronen Nissenbaum, President and CEO, Dan Hotels)

There is a movement towards thinking local again as well as global. Hospitality is a business which can be both, a global brand that can act locally, with care, in service.

As will be outlined in the next chapter, there has been a conflict between the evolution in business models and maintaining a focus on people. Investors in the future will take the lead from the changes taking place in public priorities and the renewal of major values. There will be more pressure placed on organizations to really invest in sustainability and in contributing to social good.

At the same time, there is a growing recognition that just as leaders need to think about their external responsibilities, so do they need to provide more active support to the development of emerging leaders. A chasm between the generations has emerged, one which does need to be bridged.

Where Have All the Emerging Leaders Gone? Why Aren't They Breaking Through?

In recent years, there have been record numbers of company boards asking: "Where are the next generation of leaders and why are they not breaking through?" The causes have been well debated in many companies all across the world. One of the most common answers is that many professionals today seem to do exactly as they are instructed, with less genuine hunger to make a difference. This is undoubtedly intertwined with an increased fear of failure on a personal level and also far less questioning and self-expression.

Some argue that the cause lies with the Education system which has been producing ever greater results but at what cost, it is asked? Are the young being taught to use their initiative and to take risk? Is there less focus on character development and more on exam results? Is a well balanced student with strong social skills of less importance than the results they attain? Have results for schools become more important than the long-term welfare of the student?

Others argue that it is the business environment which is to blame. It has become too process driven, with ever less focus seemingly on people. Many will argue that HR (Human Resources) has moved from focusing on the development of the human asset to almost becoming a legal adviser to protect companies from their human asset. They argue it is small wonder that there has been declining trust in the workplace. Too often HR has become almost transactional rather than holding boards to account for their actions in this area. Some argue that internal processes have created barriers that hinder any personal initiative. Many argue that the Industry is becoming more diverse, inclusive and progressive through social pressure rather than being a genuine industry of choice. The opportunity for HR and for the Industry to change tact and ensure that the Industry really does attract and nurture talent from all pools and breaks down barriers to progress.

Change is inevitable as the new emerging generations possess strong idealism at their heart. There was too a strong idealism that lay at the heart of rebuilding economies after the Second World War and maybe a better illustration was in the 1960s which did see a whole new narrative emerge, talking of ideals which had never been spoken of previously through The Beatles, The Rolling Stones and events such as Woodstock and the Rock Revolution.

The major difference with millennials is that it arguably is the first generation ever which believes in equality between gender and race. This is a major shift in mentality.

The attitude of the millennial generation, which will have most impact on the daily lives, is the distinctive belief that there are no inherently male or female roles in society. This belief stems directly from millennials' experience growing up in families in which the mother and father took on roughly equal responsibilities for raising their children. The baby boomer generation was the first whereby often both parents held roles and had their own incomes.

Baby boomers take a lot of criticism but in truth, they are the generation which did free up the role of women. Baby boomers were just as idealistic as those in the emerging generations. The difference is that the Baby boomers grew up in an era which saw tough recessions—the early 90s, the 2008 crash and now Covid-19's impact—and were the first to be able to attain genuine wealth. After growing up in a tougher decade in the 1970s, they were prepared to work hard and to compete to build wealth.

The millennials grew up believing in the ideals given to them by their parents who at heart did believe in a better world. As is natural, the millennials are just a reflection of the baby boomers at home.

Today's emerging generation enter the workforce on an equal footing with a natural belief in gender neutrality which will force major changes in the work place, a change that many have wanted.

The biggest difference is that today's millennial women refuses to accept any restrictions, based on their gender or color, on what they might be allowed to do and what they may be able to achieve. They believe that they should be free to achieve whatever their ability allows. This is maybe the first generation to be able to have such a strong belief.

One can also argue that the growth of AI has naturally led to an increase in automated systems which often encourages a corporate arrogance with less respect for individuals. People have become commodities; respect has fallen, and trust has naturally been a casualty.

So what has been the most influential factor?

The answer is probably a mixture of all the above coming together. There is no doubt that school results have become too important in the eyes of parents, schools, and teachers—results have become more important than character. However, research is indicating that we may have brighter talent entering the work place but strength of character and robustness in adversity has declined. Is there a connection?

A recent number of reports have noted that there has been a rise in mental health issues, mainly stress, coupled with an increased worry over financial matters. Just as business models have been pushed to their boundaries, as leaders have arguably become more single minded in approach, so stress, and then fear, has increased within business life. It could be a coincidence, but it is unlikely. Add all the above factors together from education, increased process to high pressure models and a clearer picture begins to emerge.

It is no surprise that there is a growing call for a more balanced, multi-layered approach to leadership to emerge but what is needed to ensure that it can take place in the modern environment?

Leadership does impact on the psychology of its company culture and people. Leadership needs to have a focus that is both internal and external as well as having a focus on how it can make a difference. It also needs to be grounded and possess a strong set of values. One can easily spot the best teams, in sport or business, in how they support each other during moments of high stress and crisis. It is an old saying that "anyone can lead in the good times, but can you lead when everything is against you?"

The best teams often include difficult characters and others who challenge thinking. Many of the greatest teams were not filled with strong friendship but highly able, skilled professionals who effectively played a role. Many of the best leaders have not followed the standard rulebook but instead have trusted their own instincts.

This has happened in sport, for example, the All Blacks rugby team created two mantras as they became arguably the best team in history.

1. Better people = better players. The more the players were exposed to real life and other interests, the more they thought for themselves. They expressed themselves and became better decision makers when they were playing.
2. The "no d*ckheads" policy. A player could not be an egoist off the pitch and a team player on the pitch. The Captain, the great Richie McCaw, would sweep the dressing room floor to both illustrate humility and also to ensure that everyone was grounded in their principles. If one of the world's greatest players could take the time to show care so could everyone else. (9)

It worked for the All Blacks and made them one of the greatest sports teams in history. However, the real game changer for them was helping the players to think in a calmer manner under pressure. Pressure has become a bigger issue as many today seem to struggle that bit more in the big moments, rewards have become bigger so then naturally everything intensifies.

When the NZ All Blacks lost to France in the RWC 2007, it is reported that the management team believed that the players were so intense about their play that, in moments of pressure, they were unable to see a bigger picture and remain calm. To change this psychology, they organized for each of the players to have an involvement in an outside organization with the view of bringing greater perspective and balance to their lives. This was to illustrate to the players that although rugby was almost a religion to them, there are other important things in life too. The result was a more mature approach to the game, and it did impact on performances in the big moments within games. The team subsequently went on to win the next two World Cups in 2011 and 2015.

In the final of 2011, their inspirational leader and captain even played in a number of games with a broken foot as he understood his responsibility to hold the team together, to show leadership despite his own personal pain. They all believed in something bigger than themselves and worked together to achieve that goal, and were prepared to make sacrifices to achieve that goal.

Steve Hansen, the Coach of the NZ All Blacks in 2011, reflected in 2020 on this period and said of Richie McCaw:

"Remarkably, even though he knew something was wrong, Hansen told Wales Online he wasn't aware of the extent of McCaw's suffering, because the coaching staff didn't want to know, and McCaw didn't want to fess up."

"Our skipper had two broken bones in his foot. We didn't know they were broken because we didn't ask. We didn't want to know, and he didn't want to say," Hansen said.

"What he did in that tournament was phenomenal. Mentally, he would be the toughest bloke I have had anything to do with in my coaching career. I think he's the best rugby player the world has ever seen." (10)

It is arguably the greatest change over the last one hundred years, an erosion in the central belief and understanding that one should make sacrifices for a greater good. It is a language that few talk today. Words such as honor and duty have gradually been eroded until they seem old fashioned, but the concept behind them does still hold strong and is once again becoming popular.

Pause for a moment and ask yourself the question, what would you feel strongly enough about so that you would be prepared to sacrifice something of real value? What principle or value would you be prepared to stand up for, argue for, and campaign for?

The decline has only taken place since the mid-1980s. Up to that time, there had been a consistent regularity of protest marches which were strong and live examples of freedom of speech in action. It has long been a core principle in western culture and yet had seen a decline from 1985 through to recent times, bar the Iraq war marches in 2003.

The baby boomers grew up in an age of protest marches but there was a shift in the mid-to-late 1980s which saw a movement toward greater interest in the "self" over the common good. It lay the ground for strong economic performance and greater wealth but as it is with most things, has the pendulum swung too far away from a good balance and is there a need to swing back?

The developments in AI and technology have allowed businesses to cut costs and be far more efficient and controlled. There is a strong view that those that emerged into the workforce in the late 1990s and early 2000s came into booming markets and, many found progression and promotion with ease without the knowledge base of previous generations.

How does this relate to business and to hospitality?

One of the common critiques of the modern business environment today is that as work is influenced to a far greater extent by technology and AI, there are many who are far narrower in their thinking and approach than in previous eras. It has even been estimated that the actual knowledge level of a senior executive today is 30 percent less than it was in previous times (11). Even the Bank of England acknowledged in 2017 that many of its forecasts of the impact of the Brexit referendum in 2016 were inaccurate as their own thinking had been too narrow (12). This was true of organizations all across the business sector. Perspective and objectivity have become of increasing value and are in declining evidence.

In Hospitality, it goes another step further as the industry does have a broad social role to play, and it does, as history has proven, have a need to be constantly inventive and evolving. It requires a breadth of thinking and it does need good leaders as often the teams working within the industry are multicultural and diverse, and need a leader who can bring them together.

CHAPTER 2

Trust Is the Foundation Stone of Everything

Leaders are the central focal points of business. They are the heroes and the villains of the business world. It is often the chief executive officers (CEOs) who lead the major business stories, carry the most respect, and sometimes, the ones left humiliated and alienated. It is the leaders who are able to motivate companies and teams to excel, to go the extra mile. It is leaders who do make a difference.

Leaders can be of a moment and very often find themselves both hero and villain at different times under their tenure. Consider the story of Philip Green, once hailed as the King of the High Street with the success of Arcadia in the 1990s and 2000s, but who later found himself vilified for his business practices and with the *Me Too* movement.

He became a topic of debate in the Parliament, as he was stripped of his knighthood (2016) and found the movie *Greed* (2020 with Steve Coogan) loosely based upon him. It must have been difficult for a man who was once feted as almost legendary to find himself instead vilified and discredited. One moment one has a legacy, and in the next, it has been eroded and tarnished. The truth was Green found himself a man no longer in tune with the time as the world moved on. What had been deemed acceptable in one era was suddenly unacceptable in another.

Earlier, it was mentioned that often human weakness is forgivable and can even be a good thing; but selfishness and greed have never been good traits in a leader. This was the base of the story in the 1980s with the film *Wall Street*, (Gordon Gekko) (1987), the story of Harvey Weinstein's fall from grace, which was not just about the abuse of power or women but selfishness and greed too. It was behind the fall and disgrace of President Nixon back in the 1970s. Leaders need to aspire to something more, something bigger than just something that is seen every day. If not, it sullies the concept of leadership, and the fall is more painful than the rise is good, as one has to live far longer with question marks linked to one's name than arguably time as a leader. The average tenure of a CEO is around 6–7 years. The average age of a CEO has risen in the last decade to 59 and for a C-Suite Director it is 55–56 years (13).

This logically means that a CEO may enjoy seven years in tenure and maybe 15 or more in regret afterward.

A different stance on the issue and an example of how respect for leadership can be lost through a distrust in honesty is the story of Tony Blair. When he became prime minister in 1997, winning with a landslide, he had the power to create genuine change. There were many within the world of politics who believed that it could be the start of a new golden era. The outgoing Conservative government, under John Major, had been ravaged by scandals and examples of hypocrisy. People all across the country looked toward the charismatic new prime minister who spoke of high principles and values. Blair was a highly able political operative who could speak with real skill and debate with the fiercest opponent. He was ably supported by a highly skilled team in the likes of Gordon Brown, Alastair Campbell, and Peter Mandelson.

The problem for Blair was that he was a centralist, not a true socialist in the mould of Gordon Brown who soon jockeyed for position and power almost constantly. The two were political heavyweights, the greatest political talents of their generation, but too often, they were at odds behind the scenes. Although many enjoyed the power that Blair brought to the Labour Party with three election wins, there was a growth in cynicism about the man's true values. Many felt that he placed power and winning before principle.

However, with the Iraq War came a major erosion in trust to the level that Blair became a discredited figure by the start of this decade. In fairness, he has been discredited to a level that is arguably too deep and unfair, but this is because he held such an opportunity in his hands and did not take it. Few leaders can ever recover once trust is granted and then lost.

Is it any different with George W Bush and Dick Cheney? Will history be kinder on them? The 2018 film *Vice* suggests not as it painted Cheney as being scheming, self-absorbed, and happy to sacrifice even his own daughter's well-being for his own ambition. With increased transparency in daily life, the desire today is for genuine, authentic leaders and leadership. A leader has an emotional relationship with those that he leads, and it needs to be constantly in credit.

However, if one places a different perspective on the above, one has to note that both Blair and Clinton seem to have lost their charisma and strength with the loss of power. Both seem to be almost lesser men post power; whilst in contrast, one can argue that George W has found respect with the way he spoke at his father's funeral and his general dignity in his post-president years. There are many who even argue that George W may have been a better president if he had been without Cheney and Rumsfield.

Maybe one of the most astute political moments of the 1990s was Nelson Mandela placing aside own personal views to embrace and support the South African Springboks at the Rugby World Cup in 1995. The Springboks had long been a symbol of the white Afrikaner, everything that Mandela had fought against. To watch him place aside his personal angst helped create a legacy and inspired a nation to come together. Mandela is arguably the greatest statesman of the last 40 years. It does take a very special character to forgive 27 years, at the peak of one's life, spent in prison. However, he did manage to place these lost years to one side as he sought to reconcile a divided nation and bring it together. A man to be able to unite such deep divisions took an understanding and compassionate view that very few could ever possess without having his endured and survived his experiences on Robben Island, Pollsmoor Prison, and Victor Verster Prison. How he mentally faced adversity led to his greatest achievements later in time.

It was Stephen Covey who wrote about *The Emotional Bank Account* (14), which defines all our relationships. Instead of money, it is about trust. We all make deposits and withdrawals. When the trust level is high, because we have made deposits, communication is almost effortless. You are able to be yourself, and others understand and appreciate your character. Then, when you make mistakes or offend someone unexpectedly, you draw on that reserve, and the relationship still maintains a solid level of trust.

In the same way, when we are discourteous, disrespectful, talk over others, speak sarcastically, or ignore people, our emotional bank account becomes overdrawn as we have eroded trust. When the trust level is low, people become political in work, two-faced, and withdrawn. As a leader, we lose authority and position.

Most have all faced this scenario. Most have all failed, and this is part of learning. It underlines the importance of being genuine and authentic so that trust can exist.

Part of the central debates in this era has been the fact that so many leaders are not trusted by emerging generations. This has led to a number of serious questions being raised over both leaders and the dominant business models. It has been asked if balance and perspective have been lost.

If trust has been eroded and lost, the question is then posed as to whether many would prefer their lives and business to be controlled by a more consistent approach than human nature? It is a fair question and opens up a broader debate. However, one also has to ask; how did he reach the point that such a question needed to be asked?

There have been many articles (15) that have suggested that one day business would be so artificial intelligence (AI)-led that leaders would no longer be needed. There is a recognition that the advances in AI and tech can potentially lead to ever greater social conflicts as society changes, but the counter argument is that AI and tech can provide greater consistency and stability. This discussion has only become relevant with the decline in trust and belief in leadership.

This discussion is not new. Back in 2006, Clive Humby came to prominence with the view that "data is the new oil" (16). The value of data has been well proven over the last decade. With the advent of and limitations under GDPR (General Data Protection Regulation) it has become even more of value and important to both protect and own. The recent scandals involving Facebook and others have illustrated just how important the control over data can be.

The line "data is the new oil" has since been complemented with the phrase "AI is the new electricity," by Andrew Ng (17), since he rightly noted that having data is not enough: one also needs to understand it, and then act with the insights gathered so that you can improve future outcomes. This, to some extent, has been the realm of analytics over the last decade, valuable but not enough to cope with the current pace of change.

There are some who have argued that the 2019 film *The Current War* (18) is very apt for the moment, as it does run a very parallel story to that of today with how AI or data is evolving. History does generally follow a similar road even if the tools are different.

There is a school of thought that radically suggests the replacement of CEOs by chief AI officers. This school will note that there have been real developments in both strategical and tactical decision making so that we are able to move from a world where we use technology as traditional decision support tools to a place where we are able to delegate the decision itself to AI with little human intervention (19).

The problem is that it does oversimplify the role of a CEO to almost simply that of the two-dimensional approach of increasing revenue for stakeholder and reducing costs needed to achieve the business goals.

One of the other major dangers is that AI has almost definitely led to a loss of respect for the individual and for many processes to show less care toward individuals and clients. There has long been a gap between service and automation, which does need to be bridged for, as a base principle, people do deserve a good level of courtesy and respect. More importantly, it is also the face with which companies engage the external audience, so it should be taken more seriously than it has been at times.

As Mark Twain once said, "Keep away from people who try to belittle your ambitions. Small people always do that, but the really great make you feel that you, too, can become great" (20).

It will be a test of all companies in how they engage with due courtesy and it will influence their reputations. It is a simple basic sign of behavior, how one acts toward another. If one is arrogant toward potential individuals, then there are good odds that the buy-in from actual employees too will falter. People do naturally aspire to a higher bar. It is all about behavior and trust, so for company leaders and HR directors, the question is: how do you want to be perceived?

As already has been outlined, leadership has a far greater and more important role to play than simply achieving good results. There may be many who do believe that is a summary of their CEO's objectives, and there may be a good case for AI to be able to ensure good and accurate decision making in this area. However, the whole issue of leadership is far more complex and deeper.

Although good leadership is always naturally associated with strong performing businesses, there are many very good leaders who can be found in smaller companies where business cultures are positive and supportive, people feel happy, empowered, and loyal.

The Many Faces of Hospitality Leadership—to be Found at All Levels

Leadership, of course, is about achieving goals, but those goals do not always have to only be about achieving great growth and high shareholder return. In the hospitality arena, this is important, as there are leaders on many levels: in the great chef patron restaurants, in the many boutique hotels of all sizes, in the many cafes and bakeries that have played central roles in many lives and communities. Hospitality can touch lives and find excellence in many forms, from the corner coffee house to a leading fine-dining restaurants to a beach resort to a bustling city center hotel. Hospitality leaders come in many shapes and forms and range from a CEO to a general manager, from the executive chef to the head housekeeper, from an exceptional receptionist to a restaurateur.

It was Viscount Thurso (a former General Manager at the Lancaster Hotel in Paris (1981–1985), Cliveden Hotel (1985–1992), and CEO of Champneys Group who would talk about the *theory of equality of respect* (21), which is based on the premise that it does not matter what your position in society but the quality of your work. Never judge anyone from their position in their hierarchy, but by the way they conduct themselves and their work. There is a famous Italian proverb that states:

"Once the game is over, the King and the pawn go back in the same box" (22).

It is a simple comment, but illustrates the basis of what make hospitality such a great industry; that everyone has an important role to play in ensuring that a guest receives an experience. In hospitality, the king needs the pawns to be equally motivated.

The underlying point being that, in hospitality, leadership is shown at all levels through excellence in many different disciplines. It is what makes hospitality special; it is a meritocracy in its truest form. There needs to be respect for the great skills on display from the great chef, the leading sommelier with his love of wine, the housekeeper who make the room perfect or the receptionist who makes a guest feel that they are visiting a home, away from home.

Michael Gray, a former vice president (VP) for Hyatt in London noted:

> We used to think of guests coming to our home but our thinking changed when we learnt that we were entering the guest's lives and playing a role.

Whatever your thoughts on the concept of AI playing the role of a CEO, this is unlikely to ever be the case in hospitality. People still buy people in business and follow people who inspire them in work and in life. There will be hotels, cafes, and restaurants that are AI-led, but still more is needed.

One can argue that political leaders are not as powerful as they may seem, that the system has control, but people still desire leadership. It is not something to be underestimated. Leaders are needed both to change organizations and to produce results. It is leadership that creates the culture and its values. There are many examples of a great business led by one person, which then declines once the leader is succeeded, as culture, motivation, and message are eroded with a new voice and new approach. How many good number 2s have not been able to make the transition to being a number 1? It poses different questions, and the expectation is that much higher.

It is one of the core reasons why so many are able to reach leadership levels, but not hold long tenures, as it is not about intellect but often about character, values, and something that sits deep within an individual; their values, their beliefs, their true motivation.

A leadership role will test every part of a person's character, and often, many will fall short. This is no bad thing in itself as long as one is prepared to accept that failure goes along with the territory of being a leader and learns.

> I do believe that over the years, leadership has evolved from having to show physical power—I think about strong leaders who

were depicted as strong men sitting on horses—to being a strong and loud leader who dared to take decisions but did not accept push back—slamming hands onto tables and shouting—to where we are now, where a leader dares to be vulnerable and human, interacts and asks for different insights and recognises that they do not know it all.

(Ingrid Eras-Magdalena, EVP Chief HR Officer, Belmond)

The aforementioned quotation by Ingrid Evas-Magdalana does strike a chord as the reason that many do want to see a more open, human approach from leaders is that they desire greater humanity, greater genuineness, and are weary of corporate narratives. They have become cynical of leaders who in truth have been focused more on shareholder value than the human asset. Recent business models have demanded greater returns, and naturally, this will have consequences.

In fairness, this has been one of the challenges of the time as we have also lived through an era of austerity or recovery form the 2008 crash and still shareholders have wanted their return. Business leaders have had to navigate their way through a compromise between the two and have often been left placing shareholder value over a balanced approach as that was simply what was being demanded.

Leaders' primary responsibility is to their shareholders. However, they also have a major responsibility for the people who they lead. It is the role of a leader to bridge both, marry both. However, often, the former has been placed first. One can make a strong argument that this preference of one at the detriment of the other has created a range of major issues that will be analyzed later in the book. It is also why there is a growing call for leadership teams to focus on building sustainable business models that place people and environment at its heart alongside shareholder value.

It is fair to say that, often, too much is expected of leaders. Society does place a heavy burden of expectancy on their shoulders, so, in truth, it is no major surprise that most will only be able to name between five or six genuine leaders who they respect and admire. Even if one takes a broader historical perspective, the list may extend to 10. Considering the number of leaders that one will encounter during a career; this is a pretty low number. One has to ask if this is a good enough return.

"The leader that you will remember is the one with real convictions and values that they will stand by. They are very few," noted Peter Lederer, former MD and Chairman of Gleneagles.

For a leader to be able to lead, they need not only great character and talent but also the ability to attract a good team around them. A leader is only really as good as the team that sits around them. In the world of sport, it is often noted that the best teams in the world will contain at least five leadership figures across the team in order to be world class. It takes a number of leaders who are able to make good decisions under pressure, not just one person sitting at the helm.

It is a fair argument to say that it is harder today for leaders to achieve this as it is becoming harder to get people to follow. As the world has become increasingly transparent, as social media have become increasingly dominant, the aura of many has been burst. At the same time, the world has changed at a rapid speed, so things that were deemed acceptable just a decade ago would be viewed as unacceptable today. One only has to watch some of the films from the 2000s to see many words, behaviors, and actions that would not be acceptable today. In many ways, this has been for the good and also allowed for a more progressive agenda to evolve, but it has made many fearful of communicating in case of causing offence, and arguably, it means that many are more *wooden* in their communications and not as genuine and authentic as many desire.

> Leadership today is much more complex than it was even a decade ago. We live in a global world with greater connectivity due to mobile access and social media. There are increased demands on leaders to manage a workforce that is always connected, to manage reputation at a faster pace given the immediacy and impact of social media and to manage the operational outcomes of the day to day in a highly controlled manner.

(Martin Rinck, EVP and Chief Brand officer at Hilton in Vancouver)

The Fragile Balance Between Leader, Culture, and Employees

Of course, one of the major factors about leadership is how it does impact on the 90 percent of people who follow the lead of others. They are often forgotten in the many books written on leadership, and yet, of course, their role in the overall framework of a company or a purpose is fundamental, as they are the ones who do the action. However, in hospitality, it is often these people who are the interface with customers.

There is a great, often recounted story of a janitor at NASA who when asked by the president on a visit to NASA as to what he did, answered with "I am helping put a man on the moon, Mr. President" (23). The Janitor understood his purpose in supporting others in the team and finding pride in being part of the overall mission. NASA clearly had a strong culture that did serve to bind people together. Every role has a purpose and an importance. It is the leader's role to ensure that this functions effectively, and that employees are motivated. This may seem a simplistic point to make, but it has been increasingly difficult over the last 20 or 30 years to find the right balance, which is what this chapter wants to examine. It is a problem and balance that does need to be found.

This, of course, is vitally important in hospitality where the work of the employees' impact directly on the customer experience. We can all relate to bad welcomes at receptions, poor service in a restaurant, and how it can impact emotionally one way or another. Great service levels can only happen with effective leadership.

So, as much as one writes about leadership, one also has to write, or at least be conscious, of those that do follow or work for a leader.

This has been at the heart of recent debates, as the argument has been that the people piece within companies has fallen in value; that leaders had distanced themselves as they looked more toward systems, models, processes to almost be the key to business success. Of course, this should be far harder in hospitality, as it does rely heavily on customer service, but here too, leaders have been seen to have become increasingly remote and inaccessible. All industries have struggled with maintaining trust, with Forbes in 2019 noting that 63 percent of the employees, across the globe, lack trust in their business leaders (24).

A 2019 Vitality report in the United Kingdom noted that a mere 12.5 percent of the employees were positively engaged in their work, and that the average days lost in productivity through either sick days or presenteeism was 34.5 days per year (25).

Maybe more tellingly, a Deloitte's report on the millennial generation noted that the majority did not believe that business leaders ran business along ethical grounds. This is a pretty damning starting position. It noted that millennials are increasingly skeptical of businesses' motives and their impact on society. Companies need to take these attitudes seriously if they do not want to miss out on the younger generations' potential as consumers and employees (26).

In its Global Millennial Survey 2019, Deloitte found that millennials are not only disillusioned with the economy and technology, but fewer and fewer of them have positive opinions of businesses. Out of the 13,000 millennials from 42 countries that were surveyed, 55 percent of the respondents noted that a business has a positive impact on wider society, down from 61 percent in 2018. Deloitte concluded that this is the result of "growing views that businesses focus on their own agendas rather than considering wider society," which 76 percent of the respondents agreed with. (Millennials surveyed were born between January 1983 and December 1994.).

One of the most common conversations of recent times has been on how many emerging talents expect something different from leaders going forward. This is nothing new. There has been a momentum building, as the level of trust has declined.

Research suggests people are weary of the lack of trust that they have in leaders and want something that is more genuine and inclusive: that once again places people and society at the forefront. There is a growing desire to see people and communities placed first again. There is also a growing movement toward more progressive philosophy that does represent the aspirations of a new generation.

This is nothing new and has happened before. After the Second World War, it was said that the economies in the United States and the United Kingdom recovered well through the return of officers who had served in the forces and who had an enhanced understanding of organization, structure, and the importance of people or morale. This together with compassionate government led the way to the recovery with the National Health Service (NHS) at the heart of the UK society.

It was a more compassionate approach that led to a whole number of inspirational leaders breaking down social barriers and creating real progression. This was arguably led by the United States through the likes of JFK and Martin Luther King based off a growing prosperity within the economy.

The 1970s were a difficult era, but it did lay the landscape for Thatcherism and Reaganism to really free up entrepreneurship and business. It suddenly placed wealth generation first and freed up both business and the economy to prosper. It was not all pretty, but it was effective. Suddenly after the compassion and social revolution of the 1960s where it was important to be compassionate, suddenly it was almost cool to be selfish and ruthless. The Big Bang of 1987 (27) arguably changed the Financial Sector's psychology and thinking for the next 30 years to follow. Suddenly, new technology and wealth generation were linked.

The late 1990s, led by the likes of Clinton and Blair, saw a new era where soundbites and spin became hallmarks of leadership. Both were exceptional speakers and both could maximize a moment effectively. It is something that knocked on into everyday life.

One of Blair's soundbites that illustrates the moment was just before signing the Good Friday Agreement when he commented:

A day like today is not a day for soundbites, really. But I feel the hand of history upon our shoulders. I really do (28).

Businesses did follow with many superficial clichés being spoken in public, a new reliance on the dominance of brands with the consumer, combined with a new focus on systems and structures allied with a rise in new technology that did change so much. All together, it served to create a landscape where few could feel real trust in what was being presented.

The crash of 2008/2009 has been well documented. In retrospect, it was a natural result of a change in behaviors, a growth in arrogance that came along with a long boom period. However, during and after the crash, very few leaders fell away and much of what had been built was continued through the austerity era. It was commented at the time that as companies came under pressure, it was middle and junior management who paid the price, not the senior players. The banks, of course, took the brunt of the criticism, but many turned a blind eye to the evidence.

Given all this, it was natural that there was a growing chasm between leaderships and emerging leaders, both almost at odds with each other. Leadership teams have been highly critical of millennials and asking why so few have been breaking through to board level. The result has been a growing disengagement by many within work and many talents preferring to opt out to work for or become entrepreneurs. There has been a growing clamor for a more compassionate approach to society, global issues, and people.

The facts have long been suggesting that many established leaders have struggled to build bonds within their own teams, and that there has been a growing lack of trust in leaders.

> I think the criticisms of Millennials has been unfair. They don't understand our generation and that's why they don't trust us. The older generation grew up in an environment of respecting authority, did not question anything. Parenting styles have changed. The younger generations could see their parents in a more vulnerable place and more playful—and when they got to the workplace, they are asking the "why" question because they learnt that from their parents.

(Kathryn Pretzel Shiels, Consultant and Mentor)

> The older generations have been expecting Millennials to adapt to their rules. We should be more flexible instead. We need to provide the younger generations with greater support, a career path with strong development. What Millennials want to see in a future employer is a company that will contribute to communities, care about the environment, and walk the talk.

(Marc Dardenne, CEO Luxury Brands Europe for Accor)

In hospitality, people do still sit at the center of the equation. Yes, there are an increasing number of AI-led hotels, but people still are the dominant feature across hotels, restaurants, events, and food services. The challenge for leadership is how to bring all these groups together, for, in hospitality, the teams are multi skilled and multi dimensional. Consider the great crafts that often operate across the industry from cuisine to bakery to housekeeping to reception services to M&E (Meetings & Events) to event planning.

Naturally enough, there will be those who follow a career in order to gain money, status, power, and career development. There will also be those who are in work just to have a job. The one person who can bring both these groups together effectively is the leader. This is achieved both through a desire to connect and inspire others through actions and via culture.

A culture's values are determined by the leader, and in turn, a culture plays an even bigger role, as its sets the baseline for behaviors within an organization. A number of studies have shown, for example, that positive beliefs in a culture and a leader are closely linked to productivity. It is one of the most under-rated factors: the fact that there is a direct relationship between leader, culture, and employee. When all three planks are strong and aligned, both the leader and the employee will exceed expectations in terms of work and success. When the reverse takes place and cultural impact declines, so does productivity. Arguably, this has been one of the key factors in the poor results noted previously as there has been a growing chasm between leader and employee plus a breakdown in the importance of culture.

One often can see clear examples of how this impacts within sport. Often, a new coach of a sports team will bring strong results as players work harder to impress. In the short term, it is often a healthy relationship as the harder work leads to stronger results, which creates a good relationship between the players and the coach. Of course, such an improvement is only short term, unless the coach is able to build a culture that bonds all parties together to build something that becomes bigger than the individual. This then helps to drive all to stronger levels of performance. Those who do not achieve this will see results begin to turn and ebb away, and then, the coach's job naturally becomes harder.

At its best, culture is the unseen, emotional glue that binds people to a leader. It creates a set of values that employees do positively buy into.

Maybe a good example are those political campaigns when so many volunteers take to the streets to campaign for a candidate that they may not even know. The one thing that binds them to the cause is a strong belief in what they stand for, their principles, objectives, and values; the fact they have the ability to make a positive difference to daily life.

In such situations, the volunteers, and employees, will see their leader as better than, in truth, they really are. They tend to give that person the benefit of the doubt and take on more risk on request than they otherwise would.

In previous decades, this naturally was more effective and stronger, as today's world has become so transparent that there is really very little scope for anything to be hidden. The pressure on leaders has heightened. The expectation on behaviors too has grown, and it is natural that many leaders have become increasingly withdrawn and sought to find strength in processes and technology. Would Winston Churchill have achieved similar status today with his well-known vulnerabilities? Probably not. Would FDR have become President? Would Bill Clinton?

Leadership has become more pressurized and more expectant, but somehow, the bridge between leader–culture–employee needs to be found and made stronger once again.

The Balance Between Culture and Business Models

It is a very fragile relationship and one that arguably has not been invested in or worked hard enough on. There has been a pre-occupation with business models over the value of culture and people. It was driven by a change in business ethos. Russell Kett, Chairman of HVS's London office, explained some of the reasoning for the change in leadership priorities:

> One of the fundamental changes is that leadership has moved from people who were traditionally hoteliers, who grew up having been to a hotel school, joined a hotel company, worked their way up through the company, developed skills along the way, were seen to be managers, then leaders and possessed a lot of hands on experience in operating hotels. Those are the leaders of yesterday. Today's leaders have a much greater focus on understanding the business

itself, what drives the business, they may not even have worked within a hotel but they do have the ability to be able to lead a company, and know what to do when it comes to making improvements, when it is necessary to deliver an increased shareholder value and that is why leadership has evolved to where it is today.

The reason for the change? I think the shareholders have increasingly required the leaders of hotel companies to deliver an increased return on investment. In doing so, they have taken the lead in requiring the companies to be better managed, better operated, better led, by people whose experiences are broader than purely being greater hoteliers. The shareholders have dictated the change and the hotel sector has followed.

As shareholders have asked for more, so it is natural that this demand has ripples and impacts business models in different ways.

In the early 2000s, a very senior industry figure spoke at a seminar at the Ecole Hoteliere de Lausanne (29), one of the world's leading hotel schools, and noted that for many of the FTSE 500 CEOs, the average lifespan was less than five years, and therefore, they had little time to focus on people and culture. The primary focus, it was argued, had to be shareholder return and trying to maintain tenure. Only by achieving this could one maintain stability and consistency in leadership. This always seemed to be both a negative philosophy and one that was bound to create long-term problems. It was also a failure to fulfill the duties of a CEO as, like it or not, people and culture are part of the job. A leader has the power to select their priorities, but it does have ramifications.

There is no doubt that the role of a CEO has become increasingly harder, as everyone has also had to learn new skills to go alongside the increased expectancies of recent times. We live in an era where the pace of change has been accelerating. Companies have been working to tighter margins, have been fighting to retain relevance either among their target audiences, against their traditional competitors or new market entrants who are reshaping market dynamics. Given all this, it is no surprise that the average lifespan of a Financial Times Stock Exchange (FTSE)-listed company is decreasing.

Of the 100 companies in the FTSE 100 in 1984, only 24 were still breathing in 2012 (30). The survival factor for today's companies relies on having an established leadership that can combine a working knowledge of the company or industry with the commercial acumen needed to operate in a globalized market experiencing a fast pace of change.

Interestingly, just as the pace of change continues to accelerate, so we are now seeing the emergence of a greater variety of industry or discipline backgrounds among the top FTSE leaders. It used to be an understanding that most CEOs would have a financial background, but this is now changing, and a growing percentage has a technology or digital background, as companies seek to compete via new methodologies. An increasing number of CEOs are marketeers and even from HR. Companies can simply not afford to keep still. Organizations are grasping at the opportunities digital transformation presents and need leaders that can embrace this mindset and use it to create new growth opportunities or protect competitive advantage. Hospitality is the industry that sits almost with old fashioned values and beliefs, but is competing in a new space. It is no surprise, therefore, that new conflicts are emerging.

> Hotels and restaurants business modules have evolved, and the financial expectations have changed dramatically to be able to survive a more demanding market. Leaders have been forced to change. They have had to create new leadership styles to cope with the modern responsibilities of running a business. From the back seat to the front seat, leaders needed to be more involved with their business, to be more hands on and to be able to continually change and adapt to the markets . . . business modules are required to be far more dynamic, lighter and able to adapt within a shorter window of time to still to achieve sustainable results. Cash flow was made the King of the business and the long-term cash investments were put to sleep.

(Thomas Sorcinelli, Director of F&B at Heckfield Place)

Russell Kett, Chairman of HVS, also underlined how the overall models and thinking had changed over the years:

There has been an evolution of separating the bricks from the brains, traditionally the owner of the hotel would also operate. The management of the hotels have become more separated from the ownership of the actual assets and within the management, you have also got the split between the branding and the operation. The business model has evolved. Franchising has increased. Management companies have increased along with the ownership model having changed.—You today have a focus on each component being optimised to be able to deliver a greater return in the investment. That is the driver. How can we make more money? It is a more sophisticated business model and it has been very successful.

A Generational Shift

With overall lifespans increasing, greater wealth being attained, and the age of retirement going up, there has been a generational shift that has occurred across the market to underline some of the previous stated issues. CEOs have remained in past for far longer than ever before and, as has been noted, fewer emerging talent is breaking through.

Some can argue that we have been fortunate to have proven, established CEOs remain in place to guide many companies to greater success and prosperity. The baby boomer generation can rightly be hailed as one of the strongest generations in building wealth ever. However, has it also been a barrier to natural change and progress?

It is a double-edged sword, as it can take time for talented staff to develop into self-assured and well-prepared business leaders, and there is less space for chance. Again, one of the challenges to be faced is how to find a better balance.

As with all things in life, new leaders will emerge. This generation will need to pass the baton of leadership on, and the millennials do seem to possess a very positive outlook and set of values. It is likely that they will create a genuine momentum for change, but what this change will look like is still to be seen.

Leaders in the modern world must deliver certain behaviours, values and have a certain personality. Young people do not want to follow the old order or directions. They are asking new and different questions: "What do you do to save the world?"

To be accepted by the younger generation, we need to deliver new solutions and behaviours. A modern leader has to demonstrate a good side to their personality. It used to be very directive and forceful in style but it has changed . . . evolved to something new.

(Luc de La Fosse, Vice President Hospitality Al Khozama Management Company)

CHAPTER 3

Service and Sustainability: Cousins Central to the Progressive Business

The relationship between service and sustainability in business has rarely been explored, but the two are closely connected. They are like cousins, not quite in the same family, but closely related. If a focus of any chief executive officer (CEO) or managing director (MD) is on developing a strong, sustainable business, then this logically requires a strong service ethic that will sit at the core of how a business interacts with customers. It defines how a company interacts with its customers, in how it builds loyalty and trust. It also requires great people who are positively engaged in the business and in their interaction with the external audience.

It is too simplistic to note that there has been a rising momentum in recent times to see business shifting from the almost immediate, short-term thinking, which has been dominant over the last 20 years, to a far more long-term approach, which is greatly desired by many. The truth is that many leadership teams have understood the need, and the business case, for developing a broader strategic approach, which does encompass sustainability, environment, social and economic strategies, which in turn develops a progressive agenda and attracts new investors. It has been a change in tide that has been building in voice ever since the London Olympics of 2012. This set new benchmarks. However, it has been growing stronger in momentum in 2015 and took new twists in 2020 with how the coronavirus has also impacted.

It is no secret that many in the emerging generations view business as often lacking in strong ethics. Deloitte's reports on millennials, 2018 and 2019 (31), strongly indicate how many in the emerging generation lack trust in their leadership teams and also lack trust in the business ethics that do lead business. Millennials have an eye on a different business philosophy; one that does build stronger long-term business platforms built off strong tech, engaged employees and a focus on an agenda that is bigger than a company's self-interest: one which has an eye on its responsibility to society, local communities, to the cultural legacy in which it operates, to the economy and to the environment.

At the same time, there has been a renewed focus on the importance of service and just how it can impact on a client or customer in a far more positive manner than many of the service levels, which we have all witnessed via call centers or process-led systems that arguably have done much to undermine trust in business.

It is, therefore, natural that service and sustainability have become close allies, as both are central to a more progressive business outlook. Of course, many will argue that this may be difficult to achieve as the hard realities of modern business are that shareholders want a return and the pressures on business leaders have created a more short-term outlook.

The Power of Service in Building a Sustainable Business

The argument is that the drive of self-interest has long become a prevalent dimension of everyday life. This societal trend toward self-interest, materialism, and competitive aggression has had many column inches dedicated to it over the past 20 years. For a whole variety of reasons, there has been a shift in cultural emphasis from "we are in this together" toward the growing culture of "me." Many point toward social media as heightening the emphasis, and interestingly, one can see that there are those journalists who have moved from being commentators and observers to viewing themselves as modern "Bernstein's and Woodward's," all out to break the story or be the voice that people listen to. Some argue that the media has been losing the trust of the masses at the same rate that the egos of many reporters have grown.

There is some truth in this argument, but it also has more to do with the 24/7 nature of today's media, which creates a constant pressure on having engaging stories to tell and sell. It is nigh on impossible and, of course, will have its own ramifications.

It is the same with business. Business is expected to perform strongly consistently and with very little space for error or mistake. It all creates a naturally stressful pressure cooker; so, how can this be adjusted in a sensible manner that allows new philosophies to emerge and grow?

Many have been arguing that self-interest will always jeopardize long-term organizational progress and strategy. If self-interest lies at the heart, then so does rhetoric with little supporting action, and this naturally hinders real progress in many areas plus serves to alienate both internal and external audiences.

Is this what has happened in media too? There does appear to be a clear parallel.

At the time of writing, we are presently being severely impacted all across the globe by Covid-19, and it is the hope that the threat of the virus and lockdown do serve to create a genuine change in how many do view daily life and the world. Whether this does happen for longer than just the short term is yet to be seen, but there is evidence pre the crisis that many had felt that the *me* culture had gone too far and had created too many social issues, which were becoming harder to solve. There was already a growing momentum demanding a change in approach.

So, How Can This Be Achieved?

At the heart lies a need to create a genuine purpose in business, one which is bigger than just the immediate. This has long been a major discussion, as many operating models have become too dominated by the desire for better and more immediate returns. However, a sustainable business model is about being more than a focus on quarterly reports.

Leaders need to embrace a purpose beyond themselves and the immediate pressures. It is logical to argue that if a business can develop a stronger *fan* base, then, of course, results are able to stay strong as a business platform is developed. However, to create the fan base requires a service ethic that really can impact on the customer to a level beyond others.

For hospitality, there is already a social role that it can play if it so desires. It can lead and provide a service across all communities and in society. There are many during the coronavirus crisis who have stepped up and shown exactly this desire. It is an old saying that "anyone who enters

hospitality must have a love of people and a desire to make people happy."
It does sit at the very core of hospitality. Just as doctors are motivated to
save lives, lawyers motivated by a need for justice, accountants to translate
figures effectively, so hospitality is about firstly making people find care
and comfort.

It has played a central social role for all the ages. The coffee houses of
the 1700s dominated in the great old cities. Then, the gentleman's clubs
and the local pubs. The great old nightclubs of the wartimes brought
much escape and solace from the sadness of war. Even in modern times,
the leading sitcom of the 1980s, Cheers, was based in a bar. The leading
one of the 1990s, Friends, in a coffee house.

Hospitality is central in society and has its role to play. The industry
just has not often made the most of the argument.

The Purpose of Leaders

Most leaders will naturally express a desire to build a long-term sustainable business. For most, it is, of course, about wealth creation, but most
will also have an eye on their legacy. Any leader will know that they will be
defined by how the business is viewed and performs over a period of time.
A legacy is achieved through good performance year after year.

It is, therefore, understandable, that most will want to create, serve,
build, and improve in the service of a broader and more long-term goal.

It is this sense of meaningful contribution, which is the reason people
get satisfaction out of mentoring and teaching others. However, many
leaders suppress this desire in order to serve more practical, short-term
objectives. People want to serve others, but for many reasons, often end
up serving only their own more immediate agenda.

For a company to build a strong, long-term business in hospitality,
then the power of service does need to sit at the heart. After all, it does
sit at the heart of the natural psychology that many within hospitality
do possess. However, it goes well beyond hospitality and can impact on
any business. Leadership development, after all, is meant to improve how
executives serve their teams, their customers, their organizations, and
themselves. However, far too many people have been conditioned to take
care of themselves first, whether for survival, financial reward, or an ego

boost. The pendulum must swing in the other direction. Leaders need to experience the power of selfless service and of subjugating one's own needs to a larger purpose.

When combined, purpose and service are the fuel for transformation. As Winston Churchill said, "If the human race wishes to have a prolonged and indefinite period of material prosperity, they have only got to behave in a peaceful and helpful way toward one another" (32). Service to others is more than just a nice thing to do. It inspires deep, lasting change and, of course, a legacy.

During 2019 and early 2020, there has been a growing understanding that if a company wants to attract the best people and talent, then they need to act and operate in a stronger more socially aware and sustainable manner. Rather than threaten results, it arguably makes a company more competitive. Leaders have been forced to start to think more broadly as market dynamics have demanded so.

On this basis, many companies started to create strategies that focused on their becoming increasingly economically, environmentally, and socially responsible—and in turn creating a more sustainable business model.

There was a very strong business case for the change:

- Global sustainable investment is up tenfold since 2004 and stands in 2020 at 30 trillion U.S. dollars.
- Marketplace dynamics have been changing as have regulations plus societal demand.
- Sustainability today impacts on relationships with investors, shareholders, the communities in which companies are based and on the people who are employees.
- Generational shift—the leading young talent will join those companies that possess values and beliefs that are aligned to their own.

Interestingly, the recent crisis has highlighted such examples:

1. **Support of the community as a path to leadership growth.** Most organizations donate financially to any number of worthy causes.

Sometimes, these causes align with a core business. Food companies often address hunger charities and the COVID crisis showed how many causes really came to the fore to help the vulnerable. Many of the leading financial institutions have started to really be actively involved within their communities, as it both attracts the best talent who want to be involved with companies who do contribute and changes the poor image that many had after the crash of 2008/2009 and during the austerity era. However, today, it needs to be far more than just a donation of funds. It needs to be active involvement. There is nothing wrong with donations, but it does not create an emotional connection between employees and the cause. There has also been a growing cynicism that has emerged over those companies, which do donate but more to be able to box tick and say that they have donated rather than actually caring about a cause.

As noted, this was already changing and companies were now investing into key projects for the reasons outline. The coronavirus took this to another level, highlighted the plight of the vulnerable all across society.

Many employees found themselves volunteering for causes that they did believe in and CEOs found that their people found a real sense of pride in how both they and their companies were behaving in a time of crisis.

Many leaders have started to talk more openly their own role in investing back into communities. Companies today are crossing old forbidden lines as they now do want to play an active role in the lives of communities and their people.

2. **A renewal of leadership as service for others before self.** Service leadership is, first and foremost, about putting aside personal concerns to prioritize the needs of others. Politics has long been about public service. In past times, many would enter politics once they had had a successful career. However, over the years, many became career politicians, and this created an erosion of the concept of public service. Leadership should always be more than just about one's self. It needs to be about those that a leader represents and not just

the shareholders, although clearly this is a primary group that will determine a leader's tenure. It should, though, also be about employees and clients or customers. During the COVID crisis, many companies stripped back their strategies and returned to core values: the *why* for the business existing. They understood that today's demand is for the genuine and authentic message and every company needed to have a clear mission that their clients would understand.

3. **Inspiring others to serve.** Many experts today argue that a successful brand must be genuine and authentic, possess a mission that the customer understands, and is engaged with. Service is key to this. The retail chain Pret a Manger really raised the bar in how customers were served and were rewarded with greater loyalty. Their customer ethos was almost unmatched on the High Street. Service leadership should be focused on overall mission in how can it inspire and serve others through actions. There are many examples of brands who have been seen as self-serving organizations, driven strictly by profitability, which have exceeded the expectations of their shareholders. However, to truly activate strategy and transform organizations, a sense of broader purpose and service should be part of the equation. Although the bottom line is a fundamental in all business, it is people's desire to make a contribution that is more meaningful, sustainable, and enduring.

4. **Service.** As has been outlined, many want to provide a service to others. It is a central plank in hospitality and well beyond.

These do reflect the thinking and desire of the new emerging generations who want to be valued as individuals, possess a strong global conscience, as well as having an eye on the long term. These two topics, service and sustainability, therefore, do and should sit at the heart of all hospitality strategies.

There is a new thinking emerging across hospitality; one that does make this an exciting period to be working within the industry. At the heart of the discussion to follow lies a core concept that suggests that operations need to possess a customer-friendly approach that creates genuine experiences that make the guest feel valued and confident.

To achieve this requires two central planks.

- An operation whose approach reflects the desires and aspirations of the guests.
- The ability to connect with each guest. Many in industry have one of two views that govern how they behave. Firstly, many view the guest as entering their premises, their homes, and their role is to host the guest, and it is for the guest to follow their rules. The second, see that their role is to enter the guest's lives, that they are the guest, and their role is to ensure that they enrich the guest's stay.

These core planks ensure that both sustainability and service do sit at the center of many strategies and emerging philosophies.

The industry is truly world class and is made up of a great variety of operations from the chef patron restaurant to the country hotel to the major city center destination to beach resorts to nightclubs, casinos, casual dining, branded operations, and beyond. The two core common denominators are essentially how they make a guest feel and if the operation appeals to their own aspirations. It is a deeper and more complex subject that many realize, but also simple at the same time. How do you make a guest connect with you?

The world today is inclusive and diverse. It asks a whole new set of questions of how we achieve this goal. It can no longer just be about words, but needs to be about progressive and proactive deeds and actions.

The lockdown period has arguably changed much. How long this change will last, time will tell, as it is arguably up to us, but all across the world, many have felt reconnected with themselves. There have been inspirational stories of real communities coming together and thousands of stories of how neighbors have started to talk to each other in a way that they never did previously. New friendships have been formed personally, and others formed or reignited through e-mail and video chats. Many have written of how they have had the time to write to people who were on the fringes of their lives and have since become central players with almost daily chats now taking place. These are friendships that are likely to never have been formed without the time to spend, making the effort, and finding out about one another. There are also thousands of stories of families that have really come together and of children flourishing with having both parents at home and actively present.

There has been a lot written in recent times about the high levels of stress at work, the disengagement of young talent, all the problems that our society and businesses face, but maybe social cultures do also have much to be proud about. Maybe the crisis has allowed many to find their true selves again.

The argument and cynicism exists that is they will all revert to type once business is back to normal and time will tell. There will be many that argue otherwise. Politicians have thrown mud at each other; the media has created many dramas and pointless stories, but maybe the real story— at least for now—is that the people, all across the world, have stood up for each other and shown themselves to be bigger than political rhetoric and agendas.

Hospitality is a reflection of society. One of the genuine opportunities that the hospitality industry does possess is how it can be the center point of communities and be able to play a major social role in bringing communities together again. Maybe from this crisis, there are also lessons that can be learned in terms of how it can be a focal point.

Hospitality is about being hospitable and caring for the well-being of others. It is about creating experiences that do make guests feel safe and create either an escape from daily life or an environment that a guest wants to experience again. Talk to anyone in any walk of life and they will recall, with a smile, a great culinary experience, a memorable night in a hotel, a special moment of shared love in a restaurant or hotel, or even a great evening with friends spent together. Hospitality is the framework that does create lasting memories.

So often, over the years, many within the industry have questioned the respect that the industry attracts from the leading professions. The irony is that so often the leading professionals will look toward hospitality with an envious eye. They see a vibrant, growth industry full of interest and great craft. It is for the industry to step up and believe in itself. That too comes from leadership that has passion and belief.

Of course, it is going to be very difficult afterward this pandemic crisis, as businesses will need to rebuild, but this is where the true spirit of hospitality can flourish and win over many admirers. Hospitality is about service and care for others, and this will be needed more than ever post lockdown.

Empathy at Its Heart

It is an old saying that "anyone who enters hospitality must have a love of people and a desire to make people happy." It does sit at the very core of hospitality. Many industry leaders have compared the role of hospitality to that of a theater where the employees are like actors and actresses whose role is to bring satisfaction to their visiting guests.

It has played a central social role for all the ages. The industry just has not often made the most of the argument. It has waited for others to argue the case and of course, that rarely will happen. The Covid Crisis is making the industry become far stronger in ensuring that it does argue its case.

As many customers seek greater experiences, ones that are almost personalized and unique, then there is a strong argument that service will once again be of ever greater importance; that many people will value those that do offer real care and are prepared to go the extra mile. This is not just in hospitality, but across all disciplines.

In recent times, most have become weary of call centers and centralized processes that offer little human interaction or care, if any and call assistants who are often patronizing, arrogant, and aloof.

There have been so many comments over the hope that a real service ethic emerges once again, and that companies move away from their own internal agendas dominating a process and once again become focused on the client or customer. The hope is also that this period will see the end of lazy service. There are no few clients who wonder if their service providers are the ones providing the service or whether it has been the other way round.

Service is one of the great skills, and too often, the impact that it is able to have on a person's psychology and day is underestimated.

It was Disney in the 1990s that sparked a new focus on service, with a strong narrative that openly outlined how they expected all their employees to constantly exceed expectations and find ways of creating a wow factor in service. Employees were rewarded by the feedback of customers believing that their expectations had been exceeded.

Disney argued that it was the smallest details that create the wow factor, and often, as an example, cite the film *Who Framed Roger Rabbit*. They would show a scene where Bob Hoskins would be fighting with Roger Rabbit, and the illustrations would not just accurately feature how a ceiling light would move after being hit, but also its shadow. Although no viewer would consciously see the detail of the shadow, it was this level of detail that would set Disney apart, and this philosophy followed them into their theme parks where each park has an underground village beneath. This was to ensure that the actors or characters would never need to leave character or scene and could easily travel beneath the park in order to take a break. It was important to Disney, for example, that Winnie the Pooh would not suddenly be seen out of place.

Great service is, of course, about detail and also about care or empathy. AI does have a place, as together it does create a powerful combination. It is the role of leaders to inspire teams to provide service that can make a difference to a guest's day.

Many guests enjoy service for the personal connection that it provides them. There is a great story of a person that traveled 20 miles each day to London just for the way one London café made his morning coffee and the service they offered. He noted:

> They always made me feel welcome and as though I was the most important person to enter their café every day. That was worth the hour's journey to go there and another hour back again. The Journey cost me more than the coffee but who cares – I felt bloody great (33).

In a world where trust has become such a major issue, it can be service that creates the basis for trust to be found.

It is easy often to see and feel great service as compared to the transactional moment when all that the person cares about is the bill being paid. We have all directly experienced transactional behaviors: moments such as when the receptionist does not look up from her computer to even acknowledge your presence or the time we are left waiting at a table to place an order.

How do you make that person feel that they are cared for and need not be concerned? All is under control.

How many times have you arrived late at a hotel only to find that there is no more room service for the evening? Could the hotel do something to earn your gratitude and loyalty? How could they exceed expectations?

As Michael Gray, a former VP for Hyatt in London, noted:

The real change in mind-set is when you stop seeing a guest as entering your space but that you are entering their lives and stories. What can you do to enhance your role and place in that story?

How do you ensure that your team is prepared to do something exceptional that will both create a lasting impression and a loyalty from the customer that may, over time, be worth many thousands in income?

One definition of hospitality is the "friendly and generous treatment of guests," but is this a good enough definition? Is friendly and generous the same as empathetic and caring?

How can you tell the difference been a moment of genuine care and attention and the stereotypical "have a nice day" or "How are you today?"

At the time of writing, we are sitting still in lockdown, and one watches with both pride and pleasure at how so many hospitality professionals, all across the world, are doing great work, delivering food to the vulnerable for absolutely no reward at all—no money, often not even a thank you as the food is delivered outside subject to social distancing regulations. They are doing their part of combat the virus and still most importantly to serve.

It says much for those that work in the industry as altruism is driven by empathy.

Marco Truffelli, who has run some of Italy's top hotels, before moving to Scotland at the start of the coronavirus outbreak noted:

It is hard for Italy at this time as the country is so used to being loved and being a top destination for visitors. It is in our own soul to care to those that visit the great country.

In EP Magazine, Marco Truffelli wrote:

I still remember vividly a BBC Radio caller complaining about the overly extensive coverage of the Japanese earthquake and tsunami in 2011, and asking the radio presenter how many times the BBC would continue to interrupt our lives and repeat the "same news" about the death toll over and over again.

While a few weeks ahead of the COVID-19's international developments, with my native home country being the first hit in Europe, I found that the daily narrative in my adoptive home country was somehow distant and, to a degree, relatively unsympathetic (one *celebrity doctor* even suggesting that the Italian lockdown was just an excuse for a long siesta), and, yet, once the nasty wave reached and trespassed our borders, the public, in truly British fashion, rallied behind the National Health Service (NHS) and the frontline workers and embraced a national code of empathy display. The 8 p.m. claps being a beautiful and moving example of such emotional demonstration.

The real danger is that, while the death toll continues to increase close to our homes, in parallel, personal economic and social hardship spreads exponentially and people's ability to genuinely empathize with the wider loss of life is challenged at its core. I have witnessed many reactions to the daily *statistics* and from shock, fear, and horror, in a relatively short period of time, we have moved to increase numbness, rapidly changing to a predominant desensitization.

As hospitality professionals, we have a duty to share our predominantly innate care and genuine feeling for the other and help fellow human beings to acquire a greater sense of empathy.

How do we do it? Let us share the benefits of demonstrating empathy, how to recognize emotions in others, how to feel those emotions, and how to suitably comment on them. Let us be the role model by showing empathy in response to something somebody else has done or shared. Then, we can practice at showing empathy. Finally, just like train the trainer, we can provide constructive feedback on efforts in showing empathy: either praise when someone has reacted appropriately or constructively provide feedback on how better to assess the emotion of another person or response to a specific emotion. Indeed, as the coronavirus furlough scheme encourages time for training, why not using this opportunity to provide life and professional training on how to be more empathetic?

As the Ritz-Carlton's brand promise "Ladies and Gentlemen Serving Ladies and Gentlemen," in its simplicity, is still guiding many of our ethos of hospitality, we can practice a very human innate feeling of being "People caring for People" (34).

It Is Not Easy to Ensure that Service Is Genuine

There are many articles and books that will say that the secret to great service is to love your customers, serve them unconditionally, and to win their hearts. This is all true, but as the old saying goes, "it is not what you say, it is how you say it." There is a big difference between saying the right words and acting them through genuine and often proactively unexpected behaviors.

How does one create the difference? How does one ensure that your teams can act with freedom and with real care? This is where leadership is so important, as it does stem from the behaviors and actions of the leader.

The challenge is to create the right culture so that the culture almost becomes an invisible manager. It is a belief in something of value that does serve to bring people together and a belief in something bigger to. Good cultures cannot exist in if the core pillars are not in place—trust, safety, and belief—trust in the leadership team; feeling safe to be able to express oneself; and take a risk and belief in what the company is striving to achieve.

One of the core themes of this book is that leadership—and the culture that this embodies—is about believing and standing for something that is bigger than oneself; it is about placing others first.

One example that splits many is that of Gordon Ramsay, undoubtedly one of the greatest chefs of his generation, but is he a leader or not?

A Study in Leadership

The Debate Over Gordon Ramsay: One of the greatest chefs but has he been a leader?

Some argue that the great chef Gordon Ramsay's visible and aggressive swearing shows both a highly egocentric and selfish character. There are many who believe that he not a good advert for the industry or the profession. Others argue he is a unique talent, fiercely committed to his profession and one of the greatest of his generation. He is a man that splits opinions.

Many will argue that the story is all about him. Talk to those who have worked close to him and they will rarely say a bad word about him. They will talk of the support he has shown them, his care and friendship. They will note that his aggression comes from a strong passion to deliver excellence to his guests. It is for good reason that he operated some of the finest restaurants around the world and became a celebrity chef. One can hardly argue that he did not maximize his potential. He has been one of the leading culinary geniuses of the last 20 years.

However, is he a leader that people follow? The simple argument is many have followed him over a 20 year period but few would regard him as a leader. More would describe him as one of the greatest chefs of his generation. Why? Because people see the wealth he has amassed and ask how much has he done for some bigger picture? For something bigger than himself?

In 2008/2009 during the financial crash, his restaurants came under great pressure and he made the headlines as he talked of selling his Ferrari as he fought off administrators to save his restaurant empire. (35)

It was easy to see that he believed that he was doing the right thing. However, he would rarely talk of the industry as a whole. When the coronavirus hit London, he was criticized again for laying off 500 staff as he temporarily closed his restaurants. Chef Anca Torpuc branded the celebrity chef a "piece of s***" for his decision (36).

It was fast and brutal. It was arguably the right business decision, bar many want Ramsay—who has earned millions in the last few years from TV—to stand by his people and show that he believes in something bigger than himself.

During the crisis and lockdown, he has continued to attract critics as he moved his family to their second home in Cornwall—absolutely his right—but it never worked to endear himself to either the local population or stay true to the rules of lockdown. The headlines were regular:

"ON YER BIKE!

Gordon Ramsay risks enraging his neighbours again after bike ride to beach 22 miles from his home in Cornwall" (The Sun) (37)

CHEF OFF RAMSAY! **Gordon Ramsay threatened by his neighbours after isolating in his £4m holiday home in Cornwall during coronavirus crisis** (The Sun) (38)

"I'm reporting you to the police!': Gordon Ramsay is criticised by angry neighbours for 'bringing the virus to Cornwall' while spending lockdown at his family's £4m second home" (Daily Mail) (39)

Has he acted like a leader?

Is it relevant?

Is this all fair?

Ramsay is one of the greatest chefs of his generation. He has delivered excellence and helped make London one of the leading gastronomic cities in the world. His achievements are remarkable. However, all this does not make him a leader. A culinary genius for certain.

The irony is that he could have been and a very good leader at that. He took another ruthless decision in 2010 when he fired his chief executive and father-in-law, Chris Hutcheson, who had originally financed his first restaurant. They had acted like father and son, almost like brothers at times until things started to go wrong in 2009. The sacking of Hutcheson led to a major scandal and legal case. This was Ramsay's moment to stand tall and reinvent himself; to take the helm of the company and make it something even bigger.

In truth, the company has survived and continued, but it has never hit the same heights again. Ramsay has continued to earn high income, but he could have been and done even more.

Has he not maximized his talent? Absolutely. He is one of the great chefs, but he could also have inspired the industry to greater heights.

Is this too harsh? The answer is probably yes, and there many CEOs who have followed exactly the same road and maximized their wealth. However, it still does not make Ramsay a leader.

However, what Ramsay did instill within his teams was a thirst for excellence in product. This is what makes the debate a far more difficult one to decide upon. He may not have believed in something bigger, but he did believe in striving for excellence. His restaurants, in their prime, were the places to visit and to be seen. He created a culture within his business, which very clearly dictated that all worked tirelessly and passionately to achieve the highest standards. For this, he was an exceptional lead.

How Do We Drive Excellence in Our Business?

Ramsay led from the front. He would not accept a fall in standard below his desired level for quality and excellence. He was verbal, abrasive, brash. He also, though, had a generous heart combined with a boyish outlook, which did inspire others to follow. One only has to look at those who worked under his leadership to see the great talents that emerged by working with him. Yes, many fell out with him, but that was inevitable, given his fiery, passionate nature and the fact that he did become bigger than just the man himself.

Back in 2007, it was a common debate as to whether Ramsay had become a brand. Many would argue that he had become that big. Others would argue that he was simply a highly talented chef with a world-class business. Should an individual ever be viewed as a brand? If one starts thinking that way, is it not natural that the business will begin to lose its creativity?

So, What Should Be the Conclusion?

Ramsay is a culinary genius. He built a business based on excellence, and he did inspire others to excel in both their skills and in their careers. He has undoubtedly maximized his potential and career earnings. His is a remarkable story. In creating a service culture, he has been a great technical leader.

As leaders, it is important that the culture at the company is right so that the focus is on placing others before ourselves and to strive for a level of excellence. This flows from the leader: it needs to come from genuinely caring about those we come in contact with, and it must be at the core of what we do.

Of course, it is rarely ever always right. It is like a sports team: the team may strive for excellence, but even the very best will admit it is rarely achieved. In the same way, there are always issues in life that impact on service delivery. How the leaders in the team handle these issues and setbacks determines the culture. In sports, many will look to the captain in the moment of crisis and see how they respond, and this will set the tone.

Captain, Captain

To illustrate and show an example, there are two great stories of Bobby Moore, England's greatest football captain, who led the country to success at the Football World Cup in 1966. With England winning the final, and with one minute to go, the West Germany team were attacking, pressing the English goal. With seconds to go, Bobby Moore calmly took control, and while all were shouting for him to kick the ball out, he would calmly chest the ball, out of harm's way, glance up and hit a 40-yard pass to the hero of the day, Geoff Hurst, to score his third goal and cement victory. It was the best pass of the day, in the last minute, under the greatest pressure and scrutiny.

Bobby Moore was a man revered by all, from the average fan on the terrace to the experts, all understanding that he stood for something more. He was a leader than many wanted to be and most admired. He was a symbol of 1960s London *cool*.

Maybe the best example of how Moore was both respected and loved came from the film on his life *Bobby* (2016) (40) when Jonathan Pearce, a fellow TV commentator, talked of walking through Turin after the England versus Germany World Cup Semi-Final of Italia 1990, many years after Moore's retirement. There was a major fight taking place in the main square, between the two sets of English and German support-ers. In those days, it was generally wise to turn away as they were often quite brutal affairs. As the two men approached, Pearce suggested turning back, but Bobby Moore just smiled and carried on walking. As he entered the square, many simply stopped fighting as he passed and said "hello, Bobby," then continued fighting again after the two had passed. Pearce jokingly commented that it was like the parting of The Red Sea. For this to happen, Moore must have reached people in a way that remarkably few others have been able to do. He was one who they could respect: he was their captain still many years on.

During his career, Moore had cancer twice. The first time in the 1960s, he lost a testicle and hardly anyone knew. Why? Because he did not tell anyone. The second time led to his early death, but he still had the time to visit his first wife to make sure, in his mind, she was all fine. He never said a word about his illness, but she knew he was saying goodbye. All these stories are maybe about a sports player, but they are also about a man who did stand for something more than just himself. Many celebri-ties today, suffering from cancer, may well seek headlines and sympathy. Not Bobby Moore.

Why is this important? It is how we all behave when we are tested that translates into how we lead. We all fail at times. In fact, many times. It is how we all learn, but the essence is to strive to be the best that we can be. Success does not just happen; it comes from hard work and from growth through learning. In the ideal world, cultures that possess purpose also teach character, not success but how to respond to setbacks and believe in a mission. Service is a mission and can play such an influential role in lives.

It must, however, be based on actions rather than words. Consider for a moment a culture that is truly focused on character: humility, service, and kindness and then another that aims to be process-led, efficient, and convenient. We have all experienced both—but which leaves you with a memory and a desire? One is based on the heart of the business, while the other is based on the mechanics of the business.

In fairness, both have their place. The first at the top end of the industry. The second with supermarkets and fast food restaurants. There are many successful millionaires who have owned fast food franchises and will not hear a word against their systems.

McDonald's is arguably one of the great restaurant groups the world has ever known. It is hard to argue against their success. They have a reputation as having the best systems and the best training. Their health and safety is first class. It serves over 69 million customers each day in over 100 countries. Its success is based on the process and systems, and it has worked highly effectively.

However, for restaurants that offer great skilled service, the process is different. It starts with the leadership and flows up through the team to the guests. No one can expect a team to live out the spirit of hospitality in service of others if the culture and leadership teams do not walk the talk ourselves. It goes back to the Disney example; it is all modeled through everyone striving each day to achieve excellence, together. This is where Ramsay excelled too. There are many who fall short.

As controversial a figure that Ramsay may be, one can fairly argue that he did lead by example. This then walked the talk and set out the expectations for others to follow, which they did. Many of his chefs grew as they followed his example. It may be a journey and often fiery, but there was a culture set that all understood and bought into.

Training and Development

One of the most controversial areas has been the amount invested in training and development. There are many organizations that will argue that great service can only be delivered through a strong training program—and yet, across industries, training budgets have been shown to have been halved over the last decade. Many argue this is relative as much training has moved online, which appeals to younger generations, and there is a partial truth in this argument. However, history will show that long-term continuous success often has a strong training culture at its heart.

Great service does need training as does all disciplines that require a strong individual professional performance. Sports players train five days per week in order to excel. The military trains each day. Doctors, lawyers, and accountants spend years training and continuing to train in their disciplines, so it is logical that great service too often requires intense and continuous periods of understanding and learning. Training and learning creates not just purpose, but the confidence to be able to deliver when the pressure is high. If one instills purpose and empathy at the core, then it will naturally begin to start building a growing tribe of engaged customers.

Leadership plays a common and important purpose in building teams:

- Without vision, people do not know what they are supposed to aim for. What is our common goal? What do we want to achieve in business? What is our business philosophy? What makes us different to anyone else?
- Without understanding excellence, the team cannot understand their purpose and objective. Marco Truffelli, a leading hotelier across Europe, earlier referred to The Ritz Carlton and their philosophy. At the start of their day, the Ritz Carlton teams gather for their daily line up. During this 15-minute gathering, they do three things. They hear what is happening at a corporate level and what is happening at the local hotel, such as a memorable story of how putting their vision to work has affected a guest. They also review their 20 core values. These values are always within the team members' sight and hearing. There is never an excuse for the team members to not know how to respond in any given situation in order to accomplish the Ritz Carlton Golden Standard of Service. They are ladies and gentlemen serving ladies and gentlemen.

Another example is Taylors of Harrogate who oversee Yorkshire Tea, the famous Bettys Team Rooms as well as a number of businesses. It may have changed, but back in the late 2000s, they had a philosophy of making sure that their teams meet, but the meetings could only be two minutes long. It ensured that the leaders of each team had to be prepared and needed to keep their communication short and to the point. At the same time, it improved interaction as all would listen intently for two minutes, and so, it set a tone for action over words.

A similar philosophy had been introduced by ASDA's former CEO, Archie Norman, who used to have a room with tables but no chairs next to his office. His view was that if someone could not sit down, they would not waffle and waste time. It sent out a message and sat at the heart of a culture that in turn became very successful.

- When recruiting, it is important that all buy into the mission and the objectives being set. Disney again exceled in this area, and all new recruits are asked to watch a film in advance of interviews, which set out expectations very clearly. It also sets out the standards the company strives for. The outcome of training and development of frontline crew members should reflect the values of the owners.

- It is also important that employees know and understand their purpose in their position. The goal is to provide a seamless delivery of our product or service. For that to happen, each team member needs to know what they are responsible for and how to best serve in that position. This can only be achieved through communication.

One Can Never Over-Communicate

One of the hardest things to train is the importance of both communication and repetition. It is argued today that for a consumer to hear a simple marketing message, they need to hear it between seven and eight times before it begins to register or is recognizable. It stands at the heart of all advertising, a clear message, which is said over and over again.

The same is true with teams. One needs to create simple messages that can be communicated time and again so that it becomes an integral part of the culture. It may sound wrong, but the simple truth is that one can never over-communicate in the modern age.

Michael Karnjanaprakorn the CEO of Skillshare, in 2015 (41), wrote:

> The biggest lesson I've learned as CEO is the art of over-communicating. I'm constantly repeating the vision of the company to our team. When I thought I couldn't over-communicate anymore, I would reiterate the vision again.
>
> I noticed a funny thing begin to happen. People started to understand what and more importantly why we were doing things. The message was trickling throughout the entire company. People would repeat to each other what I was repeating to them (41).

Empathy

Empathy does sit at the heart of hospitality. Arguably, it is the most important personality trait that someone in hospitality may possess.

> There is another old saying that says that "people don't care how much you know until they know how much you care."

It is true. Adam Elliott (Founder of Paragon Hospitality) noted that:

> The leaders that you remember in your career, are the ones that lived life with conviction and with passion. I love working with passion, with those who care and then I have all the time in the world for them. If they talk to me in clichés and with corporate language, I soon switch off.

In hospitality, people do need to know that it is all genuine. A director who used to work for Adam Elliott fondly recalled the first time they met:

> Adam listened to me for about 10 minutes before telling me that I was talking rubbish. We proceeded to have a row—but I loved him for his honesty and genuine approach. It made me want to work for him. We may not have agreed but I knew I could work for this man.

Of course, the issue is far deeper than just being genuine and authentic. The key part of the aforementioned was that both parties showed they cared, were human, and could understand each other. With empathy, the key is to be able to understand how someone feels. We need to be able to read a difficult situation. We need to understand vulnerability, fear, and distress and be able to act accordingly. We need to be able to place ourselves away and focus on the other person. This does take some courage and a genuineness and selflessness of heart to help another. For some, it is natural. For others, it needs to be trained through teaching and experience.

No one wants to be judged for their failings. No one wants to feel as though they have failed. Can you then place your arm around another, reassure them in the darkness of their moment, that all will be fine and not to worry? Are you able to take on their fear and ease it?

The knowledge that a leader cares about your concerns builds trust.

There is a story told about a guest who called the hotel general manager to the room where he was staying to complain that some very important documents had been thrown away by the housekeepers who had cleaned his room. The client was of great importance, so he sent a team down to the local rubbish tip to search for the papers. After hours of searching, they managed to locate the papers, but they had been stained and not for use. The general manger though was very proud of his team who had searched for hours through rubbish just to find the guest's missing papers. It showed real character and desire to help the guest. As it turned out, the guest was not as concerned as he had a spare set of papers, but appreciated the efforts taken by the hotel.

Another more amorous story was of a general manager who used to tease his head chef over a crush that he had on a waitress. One evening while checking the hotel was all closed down for the evening, he wandered into the kitchen where he found his chef in the middle of making love to the waitress. The general manager simply smiled and said, "Goodnight Chef" and left them together.

Then, there is a story of a general manager who watched on as one of his junior female event organizers was heavily criticized by a client who was being unreasonable and demanding. The criticism left the event mangers deeply upset for having let the client down. As she arrived home, there was a bouquet of flowers awaiting her from the general manager with the simple message that "We may fail today but tomorrow is a new day where we may soar."

Business is business. It will have its high moments and its low. However, empathy is about placing a person first and understanding, but also meeting their needs. It is a very special skill that makes many in hospitality stand apart. When greeting a guest, one needs to greet them as a person first and their business as secondary. Service is about how we make an individual feel at a moment in time. If we excel, more business will naturally follow.

During any career in hospitality, one will see anger, tears, sadness, despair, and sorrow. None is a positive emotion, but all need to be faced. In the majority of cases, most people just want to be faced by an example of kindness and compassion. There is always something that can be said to show that person, however bad they may feel, that they do matter and are important.

This is why, putting others before ourselves at all times is so incredibly important in the spirit of hospitality. It does not matter how ridiculous their request may sound; it does not matter whether company policy allows for the required response. What matters is making the guest feel important enough for someone to empathize with their felt need and work with them to meet it.

London Edition Hotels often talked of how they empowered their room service teams to spend as was needed to resolve a complaint. As this policy was launched, there was some concern that costs could escalate, but instead, they found that their teams responded with greater care, spending less, and gaining greater levels of satisfaction. It showed that things are not always about cost, but also about trust.

If one wants to be a leader in a hospitality environment, then it is about thinking and serving people. It may sound like a strange comment, but the vast majority of people are neither comfortable in themselves nor relaxed. The majority will be anxious, tense, and concerned. The challenge is how to make these guests feel safe in your hotel or venue. If one can make a person relax, not only will they be loyal, the odds are that they will also spend more in the hotel—at dinner, on room service, at the bar. Ken McCulloch, the great Scottish hotelier, believes that his hotels had appeal as their design and service made people feel relaxed and special. It allowed them to be uninhibited, as if they were in their own homes.

CHAPTER 4

How Has the Development in AI Impacted on Leadership on People and the Industry?

For many, this may be one of the more important chapters, as artificial intelligence (AI) advances do already impact on our daily lives, in how we think and communicate. As AI developments grow, the question that is constantly being asked is how will this impact on our work lives, on our ability to innovate, to work, and within our interpersonal relationships?

As with all progression, there is much good achieved, but also many concerns and dangers to be aware of. There is little chance that it will not impact on how we lead, how we communicate, and how we do ensure that the industry progresses.

Peter Lederer, former MD and Chairman of Gleneagles and VisitScotland noted:

> "It is the role of all leaders to make sure that we do move things along and improve the lives of those that work in the industry."

It is, therefore, likely that AI will be the tool that does most greatly impact on this objective, as it has been a dominant factor over the last 20 years. One of the arguments is that many businesses have quickly taken all the advancements that AI does offer, but with very little thought to the ramifications that it may have on people, thinking, strategies, processes, and clients. Many point to the increased workloads that we carry today, the increased levels of arrogance in some communications, an erosion of respect, the increased level of processes that many business possess, even the increased polarization in service levels. Some argue that business is still learning how to manage the power of AI, but there are others who believe there are those who simply turn a blind eye to the vulnerabilities AI creates, as it leads to stronger performance.

The growth in AI has offered new and greater methods to enhance the customer experience, for also providing an up-to-date visibility on performance via data. If one visits many of the leading sports stadiums around the world, the food service management teams will have complete visibility on how each outlet is performing around a stadium on a minute-by-minute basis. It allows for far greater consistency and visibility. This is hardly rare and can be found across all operations—in hotels, restaurants, stadia, resorts, and major events. In many ways, it allows for the industry to be far more attractive to investors, as there is a strong asset base and the operations can be far more easily controlled than ever before. One can forecast with greater accuracy, and there is less margin for error.

In a previous chapter, the debate over whether chief executive officers (CEOs) could be effectively replaced by chief AI officers was analyzed. There are those who argue that AI could provide far more consistent and fairer leadership. The counter argument is that the human spirit is where inspiration, emotion, and ambition are to be found.

So, how will AI impact, at least in the short term?

There are two schools of thought. The first argues that the hotel industry will divide into three or four clear markets:

- The experiential hotel
- The AI-led hotel where the guest will never need to experience any employee interaction as check-in, the key, and check-out will all be controlled via a mobile app or similar. Hotel Buddy in Germany may have proven to be the market leader in this thinking.
- The bespoke boutique experience
- The business or budget operation with minimal service

Vincent de Marasse Enouf, Group HR Manager at Constance Hotels and Resorts, commented that:

AI gives access to powerful decision making through fast information gathering. This split between the two models—personalised/

experiential hotel and the AI led Hotel—is already happening. Will hotels become more AI led at 3 or 4 star levels? With luxury brands, there is still and will continue to be far more personalised/ experiential service in their offering.

Customer expectation seems to increase daily. Customers are seeking and expect new experiences. There is a need to develop authentic and genuine experiences in service. These should "come from the heart" rather than be reinforced by corporate brands.

There are many who argue that the industry will divide into an even more easily classified structure:

- Those hotels that follow the traditional route of providing a high service level supported by AI
- IT companies that create AI-led robotic hotels

There is a lot of supporting evidence for this as across the United States and even in Europe, as there are many robotic cafes emerging. One such example is Cafe X in San Francisco (42).

Additionally, there are many stores and outlets opening that have not been staffed at all, but all controlled by robotics. Intriguingly, Amazon's Go stores are the first shops in the world that consumers will not allow entry into without first having all their personal details logged. In February 2020, it opened its first grocery store with its Just *Walk Out technology*. One article (43) wrote:

The end result is a grocery store with no check out queues or waiting time. Meanwhile, store staff are freed up to take care of other aspects of the business like restocking shelves and customer service.

We have seen the move toward automated hotels already being led by the likes of Hotel Buddy and China's Alibaba organization.

Hotel Buddy (44) was the brainchild of Johannes Eckelmann who founded Cocoon Hotels. The first hotel was a 73-bedroom property in

Munich and opened in 2015. The retro-inspired budget hotel is built on cloud-based technology, enabling it to operate without staff members at all. It soon boasted 90 percent occupancy.

Automated hotels are still in their infancy and judging the associated *savings* is still to be proven. However, it is very likely that robotics and other high-tech amenities can help cut labor costs or resolve the problem of manpower shortages. The question is whether automated hotels can deliver the personal touch and high-value service of traditional hoteliers, characteristics that are essential for many audiences.

It is inevitable that this market will grow, and it will have its fan base, both regulars and those who visit once to curb their inquisitiveness. Some argue that this will result in removing key jobs from local economies, but all economies do evolve and adapt. The more important question is how large an audience will a robotic service level appeal to?

The second school of thought argues that the audience will not be of a high percentage as there are still many who desire human contact and service.

> Despite the development of the latest technologies like robots and AI, at our core we are a business of people serving people. While hotels will incorporate newer technologies into their operations, I don't think the human interaction of the Hospitality Industry will ever be fully replaced, but then again, I am maybe old fashioned in how I view things.

(Martin Rinck, Chief Brand Officer, Hilton)

> No group will commit to one approach alone—not without the ability to change and adapt as is necessary.

(Thomas Sorcinelli, F&B Director, Heckfield Place)

> There have been labour saving devices in hospitality forever. AI is the latest "buzzword" that is destined to make a greater impact with time in being able to automate some of processes, that need to be done without the need for anybody to intervene. You will

need to develop the algorithm to ensure that they can continue to help the guests. Fortunately, the hotel business is a people business. No matter how much the traveller of today or the traveller of the future wants to be able to automate certain processes, there are certain other things that need to have human intervention and that makes the experience more successful. The evolution of the hotel business is to become more experiential and only part of that can be done without human intervention. If you replace the face to face interaction, there is a level of distraction that can get in a way of this experience.

(Martin Jones, VP with Starwood)

Martin Jones went on to note that AI is important, as it is a tool that younger generations understand and naturally use in daily life. He commented that:

We were the first to use mobile phones to unlock hotel rooms. Younger people are better with AI. I personally prefer personal interaction. It will change and we need to have a plan. Maybe we will develop some hotels run by AI and there will be some customers that will pay for that.

The vast majority of the industry leaders interviewed for this book very much doubted that AI would ever serve to replace the human element and would serve to only enhance service and the overall experience.

There is more supportive technology around than ever before. If you can combine this technology with an obsession for service, then both AI and the more personalised/experiential hotel operations can sit comfortably together.

(Ron Hilvert, Industry elder)

AI will help to create more personalised experiences. The human touch will always be there.

(Marc Dardenne, Accor)

> I can't see how AI can replace human warmth and without human warmth, hospitality would be lost. AI helps us to understand our customers better. It provides data. Important in itself but not all there is to Hospitality.

(Guillame Marley, Managing Director, The Café Royal Hotel)

Bill Walsh, CEO with The Viceroy Group commented:

> I don't believe that the Industry will split as suggested. I believe that customers always are going to go for experience and technology is part of this experience. We are now putting Amazon Alexa into each room in our hotels. Guests expect us to deliver a service or the equivalent of what they have got in their homes. AI will help to deliver this experience, but I don't think it will ever replace it.
>
> We do need to be aware that future generations of customers have grown up with the use of technology.

The overall view that emerged from the interviews was that the majority did not agree that the hotel industry would divide as suggested, but that AI was a tool that could actively help and improve overall service levels and customer journeys.

However, how is AI development impacting on daily life, communications, and on how leaders interact with their teams?

Is there a danger that if the wrong balance is found, then AI can erode many peoples much needed sense of purpose?

The Need for Balance Between AI, People, and Purpose

Last September (2019), it was widely reported that Alibaba's Jack Ma and Tesla's Elon Musk discussed the risks and potential rewards of AI at an event in Shanghai (45).

The Chinese entrepreneur, Jack Ma, reported to be one of the top three richest men in the world, talked about how AI would help create new kinds of jobs, which would require less of our time and allow us more time to be centered on creative tasks. He argued that people would work three days per week, four hours a day, and that people would live to 120 years old. The majority of life and work would be fulfilled by AI and robotics.

The question this raised for many is whether this would be a good thing or not? We are already debating how cultures and teams, even knowledge levels, have declined with the growth in technology in our lives? Is there a danger that life can be made so safe that it loses its purpose and people in turn lose both ambition and invention?

By contrast, Elon Musk suggested that mass unemployment was a real concern.

He is reported as saying that "Probably the last job that will remain will be writing AI, and then eventually, the AI will just write its own software." He added that there was a risk that human civilization could come to an end and ultimately be seen as a staging post for a superior type of life. To avoid such a fate, he said we needed to find a way to connect our brains to computers so that we could "go along for the ride with AI."

By contrast, Mr. Ma countered: "Man cannot even make a mosquito. So, we should have a confidence. Computers only have chips, men have the heart. It's the heart where the wisdom comes from."

It does all begin to sound like something out of H.G Wells' novel *The Time Machine* when the man traveling through time found that humans lost their spark, their ability to read, their individuality, and their ambition. Of course, this is extreme, but it highlights the danger in the loss of purpose.

And, there lies the crux of the issue. Business has become a more pressurized, stressful environment over the last 20 years, with all the advances in technology. Technology has not served to increase the pressure, but the argument is that it has resulted often in making life so much faster, open, and transparent that it is harder than ever to fail, make mistakes, and grow. The one thing that we are seeing is a move back toward understanding the value of those great basics such as human contact, service, culture, sport, and art.

The real challenge, therefore, is how we find the right balance or marriage between technology and human endeavor. One can easily make the argument that if one takes away the need for human endeavor and the need to strive for better, then it will undermine the human spirit, which impacts on people and culture.

It is often quoted by many senior players that some of the best days of their lives where those they struggled through to establish themselves. It is remarkable how many entrepreneurs will note that the early days of founding a business made them feel like pioneers, explorers breaking new ground, and that fighting the odds was a real incentive. It made them feel alive.

The counter-argument is that we are living through the greatest period of change in history, as the world has become easily accessible, visible, increasingly safe, and open. That is why, the coronavirus has been such a shock to the world.

It is also true that it is no coincidence that more people than ever have turned to fantasy stories for escapism alongside movies, computer games, fitness, and food. It may be different, but the human just adapts alongside the development in AI. Whatever happens with AI, and there is little doubt that it is developing at a faster rate than most of us understand or realize, and we too will continue to adapt. The human factor will always be a major differential.

We simply may need to work harder to create understanding solutions that are able to marry AI and people or culture together in an effective way. Life will evolve as it does, but we need to ensure that we keep a focus on what also makes people excel and often it starts with self-respect and human contact. So many of the issues that are being debated today are because these two factors have not been understood enough.

It is a madness when it is reported that over 40 percent of the people at work feel they do not have a strong friend in the workplace (46). It also must be wrong when over 30 percent of the people move jobs due to loneliness. It is also wrong when so many of the young doubt their ability to have a worth in the workplace. It is also wrong if knowledge levels have declined when knowledge today is so easily accessed. We have more to do, and we need to create new frameworks and solutions.

The challenge is not to strive for a three-day week and a 120-year lifespan, but for an effective marriage that allows for AI to support the drive of human endeavor to a higher level, maybe via the creative arts, maybe via sport, via creating greater human contact, but people will and must always be the primary differential in business and beyond.

All people need purpose. It can be argued that one of the problems of the more AI-led business environment is that many felt a loss of genuine purpose and meaning which has been a major contributing factor in increased levels of anxiety, stress and rising mental health issues. People need to feel real purpose in their work. All across sectors during the Covid-19 crisis, there have been many calls for business to strip back its message to find a core purpose and ensure that the message is authentic; for this is what consumers and employees want to hear—a business with a clear mission and a message that is genuine.

AI and the Impact on Relationships

One of the major debating points in recent times have been the decline of genuine or real relationships that many emerging leaders possess and the dominance of social media. Is there a need to once again retrain many to network more effectively with their peers? Is this important?

There are various parts to this equation, all inter-linked:

1. Has the increased use of AI impacted on the fact that many are arguably too narrow in the way that they think today?
2. Is AI leading change, or is it hindering the development of talent?
3. Is there a link to the concerning rise in loneliness?
4. The best learning and knowledge share comes through conversation and networking. Can this be encouraged?
5. Real relationships and trust are of real importance and stand beyond social media contacts and relationships.
6. Is social media even to be trusted as being accurate?

The Rise in Loneliness

In 2018, the UK government appointed its first Minister of Loneliness (47). The move came as a response to increasing concern of a loneliness epidemic sweeping the Western society. Psychologists define loneliness as a subjective, unpleasant experience that occurs when the desired level of meaningful social contact is less than what is available. The prevalence of loneliness is increasing, and the association between loneliness and ill health is now clear.

In the United States, loneliness affects one-fifth of the population. In the United Kingdom, it is experienced by more than a third of those over the age of 50 years.

A report (48) in late 2019, noted that:

According to our latest research, over half (53.6%) of Brits admit to suffering from loneliness in the workplace; with a further four in ten (44.4%) attributing this to having nothing in common with their colleagues.

The study, which surveyed 2,000 British professionals, also found that a staggering two thirds (66.5%) of professionals aged 35-44 feel lonely at work; making them the most isolated of all age groups.

Why Is It that Those Aged 35–44 Are Struggling the Most?

The same trend is being shown in the United States. An article in Forbes (49) in February 2020 noted:

A stunning 41 percent of employed men reported feeling a general sense of emptiness at work in 2019 while only 29 percent of working women do, among the study's findings. **Loneliness increased significantly for Boomers and Gen Xers in 2019 compared to a year ago. Boomers** scored 43.2 on the loneliness scale in 2019, up from 42.4, and Gen Xers were even lonelier, with a 47 compared to 45.1 in 2018.

This is a growing issue across Western Europe. Of course, the fault cannot be laid at the door of AI, but clearly, there is a need for ensuring a stronger sense of social interaction, as somewhere along the road this has been lost.

Can Robotics Help?

Of course, there are many who argue that products such as Amazon's Alexa can make the difference and may be suitable companions for those that do feel isolated. This has even been the basis for a whole number of films over the years, from *Barbarella* (50) through to Woody Allen's film *Sleeper* (51) where he imagined a machine called the *Orgasmatron* (52), which stimulated orgasms for its users with no need for a sexual partner.

A few years ago, a robot seal called Paro (53) was seen as a solution to loneliness. The seal has been used as a companion bot in care homes since 2003 and has been shown to enhance the care environment and reduce residents' feelings of loneliness, though little can truly replace the role of real human interaction.

Sadly, technology has been largely ineffective in meeting the needs of those feeling lonely. In fact, it may be adding to the problem. It is logical that when we feel lonely, we desire real connection, and this is not something that can be easily substituted. One can see from trends that there are many who desire a more connected society, which seems to be on course to collide with those who wish for greater improvement in AI, systems, and technology, as business increasingly drives for efficiency and profit maximization.

Neither is wrong, but a balance needs to be found. All the social statistics that are coming to the fore highlight that society is not advancing as well as it should.

Social Media

Of course, it is not an easy problem to solve. Social media has arguably changed perceptions. Social media allows one to feel connected with a large audience. It has become a common aside that "social media is an introvert's heaven and an extrovert's hell." Extroverts by nature enjoy human contact. Many believe that introverts have found a voice through social media but it has had it's consequences. This has been a concern, as many are too influenced by what they read and receive via social media. Others are able to create virtual characters of themselves, which has little connection to reality. Increasingly, the physical, the real, and even the truth is being replaced or at least challenged by the digital, which is fundamentally changing our experiences of the everyday, and in turn, reducing our opportunities to connect.

One report (54) noted that:

- The average U.S. adult spends 38 minutes per day on Facebook.
- 16–24-year-olds spend a median of three hours a day on social media.
- Internet users spend an average of 2 hours and 22 minutes per day on social networking in 2019.
- The average daily time spent on social in 2018 was 142 minutes a day.
- By 2021, more than three billion people are expected to be on social media.
- Projections for social media use estimates the average adult will spend six years and eight months of their life on social media.
- Facebook has 1.4 billion active users on a daily basis.

An article in *The Independent* in late 2019 (55) noted:

The rise of social media has meant that we as a global population are more connected than we have ever been in the history of time. However, our reliance on social media can have a detrimental effect on our mental health, with the average Brit checking their phone as much 28 times a day.

Forever Blowing Bubbles

One of the most striking lessons from both the last (2016) U.S. Presidential Election and the 2019 UK General Election was just how out of sync the leading expert commentators and the political elite were with the common person. Certainly, in the UK Election, it became very clear just how far Westminster (and the media) had created its own world and reality bubble over the two years, leading up to the General Election. There has become such a high level of disconnect between the worlds of real life and politics. However, there are many examples in daily life of business, and people working within their own bubbles, with their own interpretation of the world, which can be far removed from the truth.

It has been argued that the Brexit referendum was won by a strategy that was able to reach younger, disengaged voters through over a campaign of eight billion social media messages. The old political methodologies floundered, and the proven methodologies failed to impact.

One of the concerns being raised is whether many companies create their own interpretation and that most communication is more internally focused than externally. Forbes (56) estimated that:

> According to research cited in Forbes, the average office worker spends 2.5 hours a day reading and responding to an average of 200 e-mails, of which approximately 144 (mostly CCs and BCCs) aren't relevant to their job.
>
> Since the average office worker spends 2.5 hours a day doing e-mail, that's around 1.8 hours spent on those irrelevant e-mails, which comes out to a whopping 10 years spent on useless e-mails, which would be 23 percent of a 45-year career.

An average 144 out of 200 e-mails each day are not directly relevant. It is not hard to understand just why the internal focus has arguably become more important than an external focus. A senior CEO interviewed for this book noted that so many businesses focus 90 percent of their time on internal issues and only 10 percent on external clients or customers and matters. The leader was an experienced CEO and just shook his head and quietly said "When did we all get so self-important and lose sight of what actually matters—the customer?"

Of course, one can critique leadership, process, and individuals, but in truth, the modern era has created almost a series of mini hype bubbles that are proving to be distractions from reality, and from the truth. It has made for both people and business, journeys, which are all the more difficult for it.

We just need to be aware of bubbles that distract. We need to find an eye for what is true.

Is AI Really as Important as Is Suggested?

In late 2019, there were two very contrasting stories that emerged, which asked a similar question: are we really any more effective or better with all the advancement in AI?

The first piece asked a deeper question. It made an argument that despite all the AI advancement, had business actually performed better since the crash of 2008 than business did, almost 80 years earlier, with the crash of the 1930s, especially when one also factors in the war of 1914–1918 and the war of 1939–1945. The argument was that business recovered better amidst all this adversity, as it possessed the two qualities that are often missing today in trust and relationships.

The second was about a *city*-employed couple that took the decision to opt out and found an art gallery and coffee shop near to the coast. The difference to the normal classical story of a couple opting out was that this couple made the decision due to the fact that they were both suffering from anxiety and depression. This they believed was not caused by the pressure of their employment, but by a mix of the endless demand of modern communications, e-mails, and social media, combined with less human contact and a fall in behaviors. They are reported to have commented:

> You can see how miserable people are and that is before one reaches work. At work hardly anyone talks to another; it is everyone staring at their screens every day for 12 hours working through endless e-mails. By the end of each day we were too exhausted to spend any quality time together.
>
> We have found a far happier life not by moving to the coast but by spending time talking to each together, going for walks and finding new real friendships with genuine people who aren't stressed out and behave with care. We felt we had lost ourselves; now we feel content.

Of course, there are always counter-arguments, but there is little doubt that there is a desire for a better balance to be found between work practice and human contact. It is an interesting question though whether business and behaviors have improved along with all the advancement in modern communications and AI?

On the one hand, business is more transparent, open, and sophisticated. There is little doubt it is more professional in many ways. On the other hand, knowledge has been reported to have declined and many are known to feel anxious, pressurized, and stressed.

So, the challenge is to find a better balance.

CHAPTER 5

Boards Have Struggled. Should They Change in Structure?

With all the statistics that have been outlined, it is clear that there is a gulf between the traditional methodologies and the philosophies that sit at the heart of millennials. It is easy to see how many times both media and political commenters have been inaccurate in recent years. Their understanding has been based on the traditional and misunderstood how often external audiences have disengaged from their messages.

It is, in truth, the same within companies when leadership teams are still following a traditional doctrine with little true understanding that their messages and processes simply are not engaging. So much of modern communications has been far less effective than has been believed. As one understands this point, it is easy to then understand why there is such a chasm between the generations. The reported levels of disengagement have been ignored time and again. Little has been done to understand the social changes that have taken place.

One needs to remember that the baby boomers grew up in harder times. The 1970s were not easy, and respect for one's senior was central within work and social culture. Leadership was far more dictatorial, and the word of the leader was deemed as final. That is simply no longer the case with a modern society, which will question everything. The processes and approaches of old no longer work. Leadership teams do need to adapt their thinking and approaches for the new generation that is emerging. The only place to start is with stronger engagement and the building of greater trust.

Many will argue that the starting place for change begins at board level, as, at times, these have been less than properly functional. There is certainly evidence that many boards have been less than united in objective. This is natural as the pressure on a board would only have increased, as the greater the chasm developed between generations. The task is now to come together and be more effective if culture is to be strong and trust rebuilt. Where does that process start?

In simple terms, this starts in three areas:

1. There does need to be far greater understanding on how to engage internal teams and audiences.
2. There does need to be a genuine desire for trust to be rebuilt.
3. The issue is that often the role of leader has attracted the wrong personalities in recent times, those focused on achieving results at all costs. Of course, this is an oversimplification, but there has been a clear erosion of internal values and trust.

The CEO

There has been an argument in recent times that many chief executive officer (CEO) positions have attracted those with psychopathic tendencies. Of course, this has truth at its core, but is mildly comical, as it does oversimplify the problem. It is probably fairer to say that the role has attracted too much "Alpha" behaviors and not enough of those with vision.

The core issue is that the role has attracted the wrong personality traits, and this is an issue that has illustrated the pressure on companies and boards.

The argument has been that the position and its power in the modern world did not always attract the best of leaders, but instead attracted those who had their own approach and agendas. It is important to note that this does not mean that some in CEOs positions are the stereotypical image that we have all seen in films, but more that the intense pressures of the role and how it impacts on others will attract the so-called "corporate psychopath." It has been estimated that between 4 and 12 percent of the CEOs do display such tendencies, which is more than the 1 percent found in the general population and just less than the 15 percent found in prisons (58).

Why Is This Important?

Thankfully, corporate psychopaths do not go out to murder anyone, but neither do they care about a person's feelings. As a rule, they are often charming, manipulative, and very good communicators, which then serves to hide their more anti-social side as their natural character is to be ruthless, and with little care for others.

The key point is that it has been a part of the modern business environment to attract those that are more ambitious and self-focused than the actual type of leaders that are needed. Why? Simply because the balance has been wrong. Whether 4 percent of the CEOs or 12 percent have the wrong tendencies does illustrate the point that there is a need for a stronger approach and balance in selecting leaders. Boards have not been united, as too much emphasis is placed on financial results and not on the overall, broader performance of a business. Business has become often single-minded and lost much of its purpose beyond delivering shareholder value.

In simple terms, boards cannot be united if the leaders themselves do not embrace a wide agenda that works for all.

At this time, there are many managing directors (MDs) and CEOs who are working with their teams on plans for how the business landscape may look as the world re-emerges from the coronavirus lockdown and how services may change in emphasis. It could well be that this period or challenge offers an excellent opportunity for boards to come together as they have not done in recent times.

There has been a lot of debate over whether board structures have been truly effective in recent times, as there has been an ever-growing balancing act between the demands of shareholders, asset managers, of clients, customers, and of employees. All this has been sitting on the shoulders of the CEOs or MDs while there has been a growing chasm as CMOs, HRDs, and CFOs who have created greater walls around their remits and are separated sometimes from these daily issues.

I do smile as Marketing Directors sometimes talk to me in their language, which at times makes no sense and they look at me in a way that suggests that I should understand and maybe I am thick if I don't. If I handed them a P&L to manage, I suspect the colour would drain from their faces. Leadership is about doing, not talking; it is about what happens between our team and the customer. What is the relationship and is it a good one?

(Adam Elliott, Founder, Paragon Hospitality)

We have written about the lack of trust that exists by employees in leadership teams, but this does not all sit with the CEO or MD. It is also targeted at the other disciplines. Many have noted that they distrust the internal communications from their own marketing teams.

Human resources (HR) has become a well-debated battleground. The relationship between the CEO and HR has not always been as healthy as it could be. Many in HR are fully aware that their roles have changed over the years, and that there are those who do not view them in a positive light. There was a report that came out pre-crisis that noted that many HRDs questioned the competence of their CEOs and were frustrated over how their budgets were viewed as a luxury.

Even if one is cynical over these results, there is little doubting the consistent research that has noted that leadership teams are distrusted by their own talent and research noting the high level of stress across all levels. If there are such high levels of stress across all organizations, it must suggest that existing structures are not effective enough, and that there is a need for change.

Many talk about structure and process, and yet, this seems to only apply to almost improving controls, purchasing, payments, job boards, and applications, which is fair enough, but there is also a direct correlation between improved controls and erosion in trust. There is a clearly a missing part of the jigsaw.

Most will accept that the pressure on businesses to deliver strong results has intensified, but structures have remained remarkably similar over many years. Maybe there is a need for change? A change even that brings together CMOs, HRDs, and CFOs to work together on strategic development to support the work on the CEOs or MDs shouldering much of the day-to-day pressures. To be provocative, maybe CMOs and HRDs need to work closer together to ensure that messaging and communications are far more effective and progressive in how it reaches out to internal and external audiences, across all diverse groups, all minorities, and all audiences.

There is a global tech product that was created to be a *best-in-class* platform for internal communications. Given all the issues and statistics noted, there is little doubt that this is a very important tool that should be an asset to many companies, and yet, they have found their average sale cycle is a one-year process as boards have simply not placed internal communications as a priority, but as a luxury expense. There is endless research that will indicate that the cost of losing a middle manager can lie between 2× and 5× their annual salary. This can logically equate, therefore, to between $150,000 and $375,000. One only needs to retain one extra person to cover the cost, and yet, middle managers are seeking to leave at alarming levels.

There is a genuine need for a change in psychology at the board level, one that places a bigger picture and objective before a narrow objective of a remit. Trust needs to start at the board table, and if this is a struggle, then maybe that structure does need to change.

Whether one agrees with this or not, the bottom line is that each company is going to have to adjust its strategy to make sure it is competitive and that is going to take all disciplines working as one. Trust will need to be of a far higher level than it has been, and this does need to start with the leadership team.

Business has become more pressured, and it needs to adapt to new processes to ensure that it can meet the challenge. Boards of the late 1980s and early 1990s were far more united than one finds today. This may well be because the pressures and expectations were less, but then even more reason for a need for boards to change.

Companies Are Thinking Too Narrowly So Why Not Bring in Fresh Thinking and Talent to Challenge Thoughts?

There was a highly thought-provoking article written in *The Financial Times*, back in 2013, which challenged whether even business schools at that time were thinking with enough freedom to be effective. It commented (60):

In the US alone, the number of schools offering courses in entrepreneurship has grown from fewer than 100 in 1977 to more than 2,000 today. These institutions hold the promise of teaching those skills necessary to forge a new generation of successful serial entrepreneurs. But that dream has been derailed. In fact, the promise of entrepreneurship is being corrupted by false mythologies.

It was a hard-hitting piece, but arguably, the situation has become worse over the years since. Even the Bank of England accepted that some of its forecasts for Post the Brexit Vote has been inaccurate, as they had themselves been too narrow in their thinking.

The argument is that there is a need for a greater breadth in how many boards think and act. Is there an argument for bringing fresh talent in? Does the role of both chairman and the NEDs (Non Executive Directors) need to be tougher in their structure so that this group does hold boards far better to account? This is not about challenging competence, but ensuring that leadership teams are challenged to a higher level so that the right decisions are made.

Many who watch the House of Commons from afar will note that it looks like a playhouse of immature adolescents all screaming at each other. There is a fair argument to this, but where the House of Commons (61) is so effective is that it is a small chamber that holds 650 members, and this creates an often fierce *arena* that will hold leaders to account both verbally and physically. It can be an intimidating debating chamber where only the highly skilled will survive. It may appear to be a bit like a schoolyard, but it is brutally effective. No prime minister would want to face 250 to 300 opponents, all standing within 100 feet without the facts.

Being held to account is an important pillar in democracy, and anyone who enters this arena needs to have a full grasp of their facts. It is, of course, understandable that a company will want to recruit an expert from their own sector and discipline. This has long been the case and argument. However, there is also a strong argument for bringing in fresh perspectives that can be married with the existing expertise within a company.

There are many exceptional talents seeking to break away from their own existing marketplaces to find fresh challenges in new sectors. There are genuine barriers to this taking place, although, in truth, it can be of real value to bring into a business a voice and intellect that will challenge the accepted norm. In a recent survey, it was noted that the majority believed that the thinking within their own business was often too narrow. This will not change unless those same companies are prepared to think more widely themselves. Why should their own teams think more broadly if the leadership teams still think the same way themselves?

It is argued today that with the advances in artificial intelligence (AI), everyone will need to reinvent themselves as they progress through their careers. Today, it is estimated to be 3×. By 2040, it forecast to be 5×. Everyone will need to be able to adapt and change as a consistent theme. Yes, this may be unsettling, but it is also a modern reality. Change is the one constant that we all know is constantly happening. The change experienced in the last 60 years, since 1960, has been immense, and it is expected to double in speed with all the advancements in AI. The world will be even more different in 2040.

However, arguably, many business models have changed very little in the last 20 years, and these are now under pressure to change. There are many CEOs who argue that their industries and sectors will not change like others, and there are numerous examples of fallen CEOs who have believed such words. All markets, all models are open to change. Change is indiscriminate sharing knowledge has never been more important, and that strategic alliances to share ideas and work are essential. No one and no business is an island anymore.

So, why is it that companies are not as open-minded to new talents, new voices, and new ideas?

Just consider how business has changed in the last decade. Sustainability has become a central theme. The manner in which business works with communities and social initiatives has also grown at speed and in demand. Expectations are constantly evolving, and the typical customer is also changing at speed.

Might it just be worth charging recruitment teams to think differently? It may well help companies handle the change that is happening all around. It is of course challenging, but the good news is that there is no shortage of great talent ready to serve. The young generation wants to have their opportunity, their chance in the same way that previous generations were given. As business recovers post COVID-19, all businesses will need the energy and innovation provided by the young to compliment the guidance of established leaders. This age should see a new alliance between generations emerge as both could learn from the other. The challenge is how to create a framework that would allow this to happen.

CHAPTER 6

The Hard Facts: What Do Leaders Really Think?

As was mentioned in the Introduction, the following has been based on interviews with 100 leaders from hospitality businesses all across the world. Much of the following book is designed to be provocative and ask questions, so naturally will contain strong opinions. However, what do leaders really think about some of the key issues already outlined? Of the 100 interviewed, what were the overall conclusions that the majority believed in?

The preceding chapters have made various arguments, but do today's leaders recognize the same issues? Do the following results reflect your own thoughts?

Do you believe that leadership has changed over the last 20 years, and if so, why?

Yes	**72%**
No	**12%**
Natural evolution	**16%**

Main reasons

Increased globalization	**42%**
Owners and asset management	**41%**
The overall business model, margins, and shareholder value	**39%**
Increased reliance on artificial intelligence (AI) and processes	**38%**
The move from leaders being from operational backgrounds who worked their way up to those with leading qualifications	**35%**
Generational change	**32%**

Do you believe that leaders are less visible?

Yes	**78%**
No	**22%**

Do you believe leaders should be more visible?

Yes   **67%**

No   **21%**

No view **12%**

Why have new leaders struggled to emerge?

Main Reasons

41%:   A need for proven expertise and experience from investors, and there is less margin for risk, which naturally leads to the selection of experience over youth.

38%:   There has been a declining focus on effective talent development.

28%:   Society has become far safer and also more wealthy, which has changed the value and focus on those in different age groups.

21%:   the generational gap

18%:   An erosion on trust by leaders in emerging talent.

16%:   A decline in work ethic.

Has the educational system been good enough in preparing the ground for the young?

No   **59%**

Yes   **28%**

No view **13%**

Is the well-stated lack of trust in leaders a problem?

Yes   **62%**

No   **21%**

No view **17%**

How important is it to have diverse teams at senior levels?

Yes   **61%**

No   **24%**

Do you view increased mental health and stress as key issues?

Yes   **34%**

No   **41%**

No view **25%**

Do you believe that customers are seeking increasingly personalized service levels?

Yes   **64%**

No   **21%**

How important is sustainability in modern strategies?

Yes   **67%**

No   **20%**

Do you believe that hotels have a major social role to play?

Yes   **58%**

No   **31%**

What are the major changes because of AI that have taken place?

- Revenue management, cited by **39%**
- Increased processes, cited by **38%**
- Automation, cited by **38%**
- Social media management, cited by **29%**
- Robotics in future development, cited by **22%**
- Reduction is staffing levels, cited by **21%**

Do you believe that relationship building and networking skills have declined?

Yes   **81%**

No   **17%**

Do the answers fit closely to your own perspective, or are you surprised by some?

The aforementioned results are important, as they make some important observations and raise a number of key questions too:

- It is, of course, important that 72 percent note that leadership has changed over the last 20 years alongside a number of emerging key influences, which range from increased globalization (42 percent), to asset management (41 percent), to new models and declining margins (39 percent) to the emergence of AI (38 percent) to even a new breed of leader migrate into the industry (35 percent). This does highlight the complexity of leadership today.

- One of the most striking features is that it does highlight
  some of the *battlegrounds* in terms of people issues, most especially in terms of diversity, inclusion, and welfare.
  - Only 34 percent believed that mental health, stress, and
    anxiety had become an issue of concern, and 41 percent
    disagreeing that this was a key area. Given that it has been
    well documented that 1:4 today will suffer from a mental
    health issue during their careers, it is clear that there is still
    a need for greater understanding in this area.
  - Only 61 percent noting that diverse teams were of real
    importance.
  - And, 38 percent noting that emerging talent has not been
    helped by a reduced focus on talent development programs.
- It is a concern that 81 percent believe that networking and
  relationship-building skills have been in decline, as this is, of
  course, a key skill set that supports a number of areas. Networking has developed a negative image and yet has played an
  important role in both learning and business acquisition or
  growth for many years.
- It is interesting that 62 percent accept that there has been an
  increased lack of trust in leaders, and at the same time, that
  67 percent believe that leaders should be more visible, with 78
  percent accepting that leaders have become less visible.
- On the plus side, sustainability has clearly become a core area
  today for all business. It has moved from a periphery issue to
  core over the last decade and now seems well accepted.
- It is also encouraging that 58 percent believe that hotels do
  have a key social role to play within their communities.
- It is also interesting to note that 64 percent believe that customers today are seeking enhanced customer experiences.

Of course, a sample of 100 leaders is not conclusive, but it is indicative of
key beliefs and perceptions. The aforementioned does highlight a number
of major challenges that the industry does face in this more open, progressive of eras.

PART II

Leadership in Society

CHAPTER 7

To Lead, To Serve: Society as Well as Business

The hospitality industry does play a key social role in being a major pillar in society, in the communities that it serves, and in the multiracial multicultural teams that it employs. It is one of the major employers across most societies and plays a highly influential role both within the majority of economies and societies across the world.

There will be many who do not fully agree with the need to lead and serve both business as well as having a social role, but there is a growing belief that this is important. It is, at the end of the day, down to what you believe yourself. It is, though, part of a shift that many in the emerging generations wish to see form their leaders. Today many want to see companies have strategies which do embrace and cover cultural, social, environmental as well as economic sustainability.

It has previously been outlined that the industry has a genuine leadership role, which it is able to play in bringing communities together: to be able to play a much needed role in society as the traditional leaders have either stepped back or lost their position of trust in communities. The hospitality industry has a far bigger role to play in modern society that is often not recognized.

How Hospitality Stepped Forward During the Coronavirus Lockdown

During the coronavirus crisis, it was many hotel and food service companies that have played vital roles in supporting the needy and vulnerable. There have been many exceptional examples of leaders stepping forward to ensure that we do show a modern compassion for those in need. Hospitality has come to the fore in so many different ways.

For the advanced societies that we believe that we live in, there have been a number of shocking statistics that have not reflected well upon Western cultures. It has been hospitality that has been providing solutions and safe spaces. The industry did so on nonprofit schemes, so this was never about making money, but making a difference. Later in the book, there are a number of real case studies and articles that have been run on just how this has been achieved.

However, there is little doubt that social problems that may have been hidden, or even partially ignored, have come to the fore during the crisis to a level that many feel is unacceptable.

- In France, hotels have been used as safe places for domestic abuse victims. France had seen a surge of over 32 percent in domestic abuse cases being reported during lockdown and acted with care, using hotels in a different manner. In Paris, the figure was 36 percent (62).
- Many food service companies created programs to ensure that food was being sent into communities. In London, it became known that 400,000 children were struggling to have a secure source of regular food, and companies stepped in to try and ease the suffering.
- In the UK as a whole, it is estimated that 2 million face food insecurity.
- There have been reports of children who have been thrown out of homes during the lockdown to fend for themselves and have found housing in hotels offering safe places.
- For many children, it became clear that their main nutritional meal in the day had been the meal offered at school, so when schools were closed, diets and access to food declined. The crisis created almost a double-edged effect:
  - In many families, cooking became a joint family pastime, and many of the young have learned new skills as well as a joy of and appreciation for fresh produce and cooking.
  - For others, their meals relied on ready meals taken from the supermarket, and many have seen their well-being fall.

- Many hotels, and other companies such as airline caterers, have given their food stocks out, for free, to either good causes helping the vulnerable or to their local communities.
- Hotels, student accommodation, and other venues have stepped forward to house the homeless during the crisis.
- In New York, 11,000 hotel rooms have been used for quarantine centers.
- In London, it was the Excel Exhibition Center that became the first of The Nightingale Hospitals. In Birmingham, the National Exhibition Center became the second.
- Across Europe, many hotels became hospitals. In Spain, a substantial conference center on the outskirts of Madrid was requisitioned and turned into a field hospital. The Madrid ice rink was used as a morgue with milder case patients being sent to hotels turned makeshift hospitals. Tourism represents 12 percent of Spain's gross domestic product, but with the tourists not there, hotel lobbies were full of oxygen tanks, medical supplies, and frenzied medical staff.

The industry has stepped forward in a real time of need. It has shown the importance of the role that it can, does, and needs to play in society. In an era where the local priest, the local doctor, and the family lawyer have all been called in question, it is hospitality, with its genuine empathy and compassion, that can fill the void. The question is, will it take up the opportunity and the challenge?

Diversity and Inclusion: A Potential Game Changer in Leadership

Of course, leadership in society is not just about the role that the industry plays with external audiences, but also how it is a leading light for its own people. It does have a genuine social role to play once again. Included in the modern challenge of leadership is to ensure that the landscape will encourage talent from all parts of society to emerge. Leadership has a role to ensure that all talent has the opportunity to be seen and to grow.

One of the reasons for the increased tensions that exist between leadership teams and emerging leaders is that there is a whole new philosophy and mindset that has arisen, one that does believe in the value of diverse teams and of inclusion, where all talent is equal and valued. This may sound obvious, but is a major step forward, which has taken place over the last 10 years, and naturally enough, it does serve to create tensions.

It is very important for the industry to become increasingly diverse. I would like to see greater change in age, as well as gender and in ethnic backgrounds. In Hospitality, we don't have a problem up to a certain level. I never felt constrained by the fact I was a woman. I do believe that you need the best person for the job and that is all that matters. What I don't agree with is positive discrimination. It is more about removing all barriers in allowing great talent to able to reach senior levels. It is more a case of removing barriers and let talent and culture flow. This would then offer wonderful opportunities.

(Vicky La Trobe, Consultant)

In the United States, 20 percent of the board roles are now with women (63). This may not seem very good, but is up from 17 percent in 2018 and 10 percent at the start of the decade. In the United Kingdom, women now hold a third of board positions in UK's top public companies. There is still a way to go, but is a step forward. More importantly, it is a level of equality that millennials desire and expect.

In the United Kingdom, just 8 percent of the boards have Black, Asian, and Minority Ethnic (BAME) board directors (64), which has seen no improvement over the last two years. And, 47 percent of the companies have no BAME at the board level. (65)

However, the number of Fortune 500 companies with greater than 40 percent diversity has more than doubled from 69 to 145 since 2012 (66).

If the *Me too* campaign and momentum has proven anything, it is that there is a desire for change, and what was once acceptable, no longer is. The emerging generations do expect to see greater understanding, diversity, and inclusion across all businesses. This does mark a whole new era.

People are the foundation for success. It is important to build a diverse team across all levels to ensure optimal value of mindshare, creativity and most importantly, perspective. When you cultivate an environment that encourages diverse perspective you also gain a culture of learning, collaboration and innovation. This partnered with a team committed to a common goal is a truly remarkable experience to be part of.

(Martin Rinck, Chief Brand Officer, Hilton)

Future books, written on industry leadership, may well look back at this era as the time when the balance was readdressed, when companies did start to reinvest back into people once again to ensure that their companies attracted the best talent and retained them through being diverse and inclusive. There are genuinely no excuses left for progress not to become stronger and more at the forefront of company strategies.

Some will counter and argue that a fall in the gross domestic product (GDP) and economies, following the coronavirus, will stall change, but the hard facts are showing time and again that diversity and inclusion do equal stronger performance and bottom line results. It may well heighten the drive toward change.

The momentum has been building over the last decade and has not just suddenly arrived. There has been a lot of hard work, educating, and debate that has taken place during that period of time. Today, all across most Western societies, the issues of diversity and inclusion have become core drivers in new business thinking. In addition to the importance of making workplaces become better diverse-friendly members of society for women, BAME, lesbian, gay, bisexual, and transgender (LGBTQ) and other so-called *minorities*, the conversation around the benefits of diversity and even the meanings of *minority* and *identity* are shifting as we speak. Even the word *minority* is beginning to lose its meaning, as more and more understand that barriers should no longer exist. This arguably is one of the greatest generational social shifts ever. It is no longer about the male–female divide, but all minority groups. Maybe one of the genuine shifts is that understanding that diversity and inclusion is not a one-way process.

In past times, the conversation around diversity was often on the idea that the benefits of diversity are one way, toward the group, traditionally female, being included. However, the hard facts have shown that diversity has been good for companies, and moreover, good for the bottom line.

A 2016 report (67) from the Peterson Institute that analyzed 21,980 firms from 91 countries concluded that having more women in the senior management ranks of a company increased the profitability of a firm. Companies with 30 percent female executives, according to the report, gained as much as six percentage points more in profits.

For hospitality, this is important as the industry does attract many females as well as BAMEs. It does have the opportunity to take a genuine stand and be a role model for change. There is still a long way to go though.

A PwC report in 2020 (68) noted that:

Female and BAME representation at each of the most senior levels has increased—Board (up 5.3% for women / 4.6% BAME), Executive Committee (up 1.8% for women / 1.4% BAME), and Direct Reports (Up 1.7% for women / 1.1% BAME), demonstrating that real action has been taken at scale across the UK. If this current rate of progress continues, then the sector as a whole will reach its target of having 33% female representation across all three leadership levels by the end of 2021.

Gender equality remains a major issue in the corporate world. Despite an abundance of research confirming that companies with more women in the C-Suite are more profitable, there is—as seen—still a gender gap in the vast majority of companies. Women remain significantly underrepresented in the corporate pipeline, with fewer women than men hired at entry level, and representation declining further at every subsequent step. It is improving, it is changing, and if one wants to attract the best young talent breaking through, then all companies will need to raise the bar still further. More is expected.

In all fairness, there has been a paradigm shift within corporate cultures, which should see some genuine change back into reinvesting in people—including investing in employee training.

There are numerous reports emerging that showcase where females perform better than men in leadership skills. However, the danger is that the debate becomes a contest, which equally is unhelpful. There needs to be a general acceptance and understanding of equality. There are many men who have become frustrated by the female support groups in leadership. It has been an important part of a process in finding equality, but the debate needs to progress and find equal inclusion for BAMEs.

We talk about all the obvious pieces in the diversity debate, gender, race, sexuality and disability but we don't talk about decision making. Leadership is about who makes the best decisions. Often this is about something deeper; introverts versus extroverts. Do we think about the risk profile of an appointment? Do we think about safe choices rather than who may bring something better and more to a role? There is a need for the discussion to think more about the diversity of the environment and how this can impact on a leader. There is a whole other level to this discussion that goes way beyond race, gender and disability. It is who is the best candidate in the circumstances.

(Kathryn Pretzel Shiels, Consultant)

The hospitality sector is an exciting scene, with a whole range of new female leaders coming to the fore as well as female chefs breaking through.

The key now is for progressive thinking companies to be looking for ways to employ and empower both more women and BAMEs within companies and in the workplace. It is no longer a moral argument; it is a proven business case.

McKinsey's most recent Delivering through Diversity report (69) found that companies that embrace gender diversity on their executive teams were more competitive and 21 percent more likely to experience above-average profitability. They also had a 27 percent likelihood of outperforming their peers on longer-term value creation. Different perspectives on customer needs, product improvements, and company well-being fuel a better business.

New Leadership to Take a Stand

As the momentum and pressure build, so new leaders will start to emerge, and they will take a stand on this issue. Together with sustainability, this is one of the major topics that the emerging generations do want to see change. Leading companies will start to show more tolerance and become strong advocates for diversity. This is again not a moral issue anymore; it is a sound business need.

The 2018 Deloitte Millennial Survey (70) shows that 74 percent of these individuals believe their organization is more innovative when it has a culture of inclusion. If businesses are looking to hire and sustain a millennial workforce, diversity must be a key part of the company culture. This 2016 survey shows that 47 percent of the millennials are actively looking for diversity and inclusion when sizing up potential employers.

By the year 2025, 75 percent of the global workforce will be made up of millennials—which means this group will occupy the majority of leadership roles over the coming decade. They will be responsible for making important decisions that affect workplace cultures and people's lives. This group has a unique perspective on diversity. While older generations tend to view diversity through the lenses of race, demographics, equality, and representation, millennials see diversity as a melding of varying experiences, different backgrounds, and individual perspectives. They view the ideal workplace as a supportive environment that gives space to varying perspectives on a given issue.

The website Socialtalent.com (71) recently highlighted Sodexo, a worldwide hospitality player, as being their No. 1 lead company in diversity (72). They commented that:

40 percent of all staff members in Sodexo are women—that's up from just 17 percent in 2009. 43 percent of the members on the board of directors are female and the company runs 14 Gender Balance Networks worldwide. What they have found is that when there is an optimal gender balance within an organisation, employee engagement increases by 4 percentage points, gross profit increases by 23 percent and brand image strengthens by 5 percentage points.

Disney came 7th; Marriott came 8th.

Procter & Gamble's (P&G's) *#WeSeeEqual Campaign* (73), which was designed to fight gender bias and work toward equality for all, depicted boys and girls defying gender stereotypes. The company has a history of promoting the issue and also records 45 percent of its managers and a third of its board as women. P&G's clear dedication to equality within its own workforce meant that the campaign came across as authentic and as a genuine push for change.

A New Era

We do live in a complex, interconnected world, which is changing at speed and where diversity, shaped by globalization and technological advance, forms the base of the modern society. It is understandable that there is a level of friction between generations, which is further enhanced by many yearning for stronger national and local identities as many barriers are broken down.

It has been a well-trodden debate in the United Kingdom with Brexit. The gap between London and the South in its economic prosperity and the general frustration and despair felt by the Northern cities did fuel a genuine social divide. The arguments that plagued UK politics in 2019 were as aggressive as seen in the last 50 years. The pace of change has been so great that it is natural that many feel lost, alienated, and even unsure. In this era of globalization, diversity in the business environment is about more than gender, race, and ethnicity. It now includes employees with diverse religious and political beliefs, education, socioeconomic backgrounds, sexual orientation, cultures, and even disabilities. In December 2019, it was noted that there are today over 60 gender identities and classifications (74). It is not too surprising that many who grew up in simpler times feel bemused and confused. Even the great social and sexual revolution of the 1960s did see such freedom and openness.

Business has an important role to play, and it does possess the transformative power to change and contribute to a more open, diverse, and inclusive society. At a time when many of the traditional institutions have struggled to change and adapt, many have looked toward business to play an important and meaningful role. It is for this reason that many have wanted business reasons to have been of better quality—but, of course, for some, this has been a direct conflict with what both their shareholders, owners, or business models demand. It has been a period of friction, as it does take an enlightened approach to see how just all this can impact in a strong and beneficial way.

Most of us know what is right and correct. We know that equality and inclusion are the right way forward. The case grows more compelling each year, and opposition naturally declines with time.

Leading Change Through Food

Interestingly enough, there is a strong argument that hospitality is leading social change, not through employment but through how we embrace the variety of cuisines from around the world in restaurants and food service.

It is food today that arguably educates societies about other cultures and breaks down barriers in a way that very few other factors are able to achieve. Food brings people together. There is an increased desire to experiment and learn through food about other cultures. It creates a basis for greater social understanding, acceptance, and learning. It may be simply a catalyst, but it plays a very important role today in bridging social differences and allowing for more progressive thought.

London and New York are both major cultural centers of the world through food, let alone any other aspects of culture. Most of the restaurants attract custom from all cultures, and both cities are a celebration of globalization. It is through food that we are even seeing cultural fusions come together. It is not just London and New York either, but other modern international cities such as Dubai and Singapore. It is easy to understand why these centers are full of immigrant populations. Research shows that there is a direct correlation between high-skilled immigration and an increase in the level of innovation and economic performance in cities and regions.

Singapore makes a great case study. The South-East Asian island, with a population of just over five million, is today one of the globe's heavyweight financial centers. There will be few who would argue against the importance of Singapore as a major center in the region. It scores highly in international rankings for areas as diverse as education and ease of doing business and has been recognized as the world's most technology-ready nation. Singapore is also highly multicultural, with an ethnic mix of people of Chinese, Malay, and Indian descent and large populations of different religious faith groups, including Buddhists, Christians, Muslims, and Hindus.

When Singapore achieved independence in 1965, its founding fathers instituted measures that would not leave racial harmony to chance. Singapore aggressively promoted racial and ethnic integration. One important measure was its housing policy, which ensured that every public housing complex followed a national quota of racial percentage. This forced people of different ethnicities to learn to live with each other and broke up all the ethnic ghettos that were prevalent at the time of independence.

Diversity and Business Performance

There is substantial research to show that diversity brings many advantages to an organization: increased profitability and creativity, stronger governance, and better problem-solving abilities. Employees with diverse backgrounds bring to bear their own perspectives, ideas, and experiences, helping to create organizations that are resilient and effective, and which outperform organizations that do not invest in diversity.

A Boston Consulting Group study (75) found that companies with more diverse management teams have 19 percent higher revenues because of innovation. This finding is significant for tech companies, start-ups, and industries where innovation is the key to growth. It shows that diversity is not just a metric to be strived for; it is actually an integral part of a successful revenue-generating business.

While most of these studies are conducted in the Western world, Asian countries are engaging in the equality debate at their own pace. Cultural shifts over the last 40 years mean that South-East Asia currently has a female workforce participation rate of 42 percent—higher than the global average of 39 percent.

According to the 2018 Hays Asia Diversity and Inclusion report (76), improved company culture, leadership, and greater innovation were the top three benefits of diversity identified by respondents. However, there was a perception among a significant proportion of participants that access to pay, jobs, and career opportunities for those of equal ability could be hampered by factors such as age, disability, ethnicity, gender, family commitments, marital status, race, religion, and sexuality.

More than ever, flexibility and versatility are becoming the key to success for individuals, companies, and countries alike, and a culturally diverse environment is the best way to acquire these qualities. Assumptions need to be challenged, conversations need to be had, and corporate culture needs to be updated so that the modern workplace can accurately reflect and support the population of the region.

PART III

Leadership and People

CHAPTER 8

Do I Trust in You? Do I Feel Safe?

The Insecurities of the Modern Age

Most texts on leadership often focus on the intellectual facets that lie behind leadership, but in truth, leadership at its core is what happens between one person and a group. It may sound very simplistic, but it is one of the most defining factors. It is about the creation of a sense of trust and belief within a group of people. People do want to believe and trust in something that will lead them to a better life; it is what politicians have been promising for many decades. People do want to believe that they are part of a greater purpose. For many, the profitability of a business is important but not their primary motivation. They want to feel they are part of something which believes in something of value and importance. In Hospitality, this can be as simple as the care of guests. It can also be as "big" as being about communities, about bringing people together, about being a meritocracy where all talent has opportunities for upward mobility.

The issue has been that fewer have spoken in such terms. It is the erosion of trust in recent years that has placed leadership back as one of the major areas of analysis at this moment. Many say that CEOs feel under greater pressure and very alone during Covid-19 but the counter is that they stand alone for a reason.

However, it is also deeper in today's world. In a world where it has become increasingly transparent, multicultural, diverse, and inclusive, the question is also asked: do I feel safe in your care?

With the coronavirus crisis, this question has been even more magnified: do I believe you ensure a safe place for my work and for me? Or, how do I ensure that my customers or clients trust that I will ensure that their safety comes first?

To attract and retain the best talent, companies do today need to engage on these twin topics—trust and a sense of safety.

> Leadership has never been rocket science. Most people want to do a good job; work for someone they trust and believe can bring them success. They also want to feel safe. Safe in that they are not just a number that will be forgotten about, that they do have value and mean something and that they are not just disposable. Many people do not earn large pay checks and they accept that but they do want to have a purpose each day and for that purpose to be respected by their managers. It is fair enough and should be the very least they can expect. The problem is that there have been too many that see people as disposable assets as long as they protect their investment. That is why so many companies do not have the trust or loyalty of those that work for them. You ask why the young move on so fast? Then look in the mirror and answer the question as to whether you give them something that allows them to feel safe and where they can trust in you?

(Adam Elliott, Founder, Paragon Hospitality)

It is a very fair comment as so many note that the average millennial or Generation Z will move on frequently. Very few companies truly do discuss the lack of trust that the young possess in them and yet do talk about how frustrating it is that the young possess a different value set to them and move on so frequently. They either do not want to connect the two issues or are simply ignoring the point.

Or, is there another possibility that leaders are simply struggling themselves with the pressures of the role? It may sound mildly absurd, but do leaders feel safe in their own abilities and tenure? If a leader does not feel secure, then, of course, this will feed through.

A recent study of 1,000 workplaces—published in *Thinking on your Feet*, a report by the commercial arm of the Royal Academy of Dramatic Art, RADA Business (77)—has found that 81 percent of the senior leaders said they were often placed in situations where they found it difficult to remain calm.

The study also noted that:

75 per cent of workplaces lack the right environment to enable improvisation to thrive, leaving workers feeling unsupported and stressed. (78).

More than a third (37 percent) of the senior managers, directors, and C-Suite said that high-pressure scenarios made it harder to prepare and express their thoughts.

When asked what situations affected their ability to relax and act authentically, 31 percent of the business leaders admitted that board meetings with very senior people was a leading factor. Video conference calls (30 percent) was found to be one of the second biggest causes of nervousness faced in the workplace, followed by training sessions (30 percent).

Small group meetings (27 percent) was also a big issue hindering leaders' ability to think clearly and act authentically, with telephone conference calls appearing next on the list (27 percent).

The study also reveals that leaders struggle to exhibit an air of calm when they feel under pressure, with not maintaining eye contact (30 percent), slouching (25 percent), and physically shaking (21 percent) being identified as the most common physical side effects.

Discovering that such a high proportion of the UK's workforce doesn't feel empowered and supported in their place of work, could be a result of dizzying pressures and lack of strong leadership, which could have a huge impact on a business' commercial outcomes and employee satisfaction (78).

There is a famous old quote, or proverb, by Lao Tzu that noted:

"If you are depressed you are living in the past.
If you are anxious you are living in the future.
If you are at peace you are living in the present" (79).

Maintaining leadership performance through times of uncertainty demands a greater need to remain present, to align your physical, emotional, and intellectual state. This is particularly challenging in the moment when you find yourself needing to think on your feet.

Under pressure, leaders tend to focus on the content of what they are saying, losing their personal connection with others, as well as an awareness of how they are coming across. In the eyes of their audience, they can lose credibility by speeding up their breathing and appearing tense, with no vocal presence—showing a lack of confidence.

This is quite a strange picture of leadership. It is certainly a long way from the levels of leadership that is desired by employees and stakeholders. So, what do we do?

Most would agree that the mentioned picture is below expectation, so it is clear that there is a need for a number of changes:

- Greater work in the development of emerging leaders so that they are able to handle pressures of the role. A chief executive officer (CEO) has to be able to lead effectively, and if this is not happening, change needs to happen.
- A different structure to support and enable CEOs? The board structure has long been the same, and yet, the world has changed beyond measure. Business, today, has to possess both a strong business strategy and approach to working with communities and in sustainability. More is being asked so structures and process of leadership, so it needs to change.
- Greater understanding of the pressures on business performance.
- Business needs to be enabled to invest back into its people and structures.

It is clear that change is needed, but it is more complicated than it may appear. There is a need for new thinking and greater understanding. One of the most striking examples of this is in relation to the *imposter syndrome* (80) whereby many, most especially women, feel out of their depth and imposters in their jobs. There is a need to create new structure in business that do allow for all to feel able and in control. Without this then, of course, there will be a continuous line of friction that surrounds a leader's uncertainty.

It was Betty Boothroyd, the former speaker at The House of Commons, who when asked why there were not more women MPs responded noting that men can stand up and talk with 10 percent of the facts, while women need 90 percent before they speak. The ideal, she concluded, would be a half-way house between the two.

The real question though is how do we make leaders feel more secure themselves? It is never going to be a strong structure if insecurity begins at the top.

Isn't Leadership Though About Behavior?

In a recent discussion forum (81) with a number of senior players, both male and female, the common thread that was concluded was that the biggest problem that business faces today is behaviors. As the world is increasingly transparent, there is an expectation in behaviors, and many are simply falling short. In a candid, open discussion, it was noted that:

- Sadly, many leaders are neither visible today nor do they value the need for integrity over results.
- That there is a lack of visible leadership for both the client and employees to see and follow.
- That, in truth, the lack of trust in leadership teams is probably well founded as many are still behaving badly.
- That listening skills to their own teams has declined.
- That many pay lip service to values and the need for real social progression.
- Too many talk well, but act with less boldness.
- It was noted how many leaders now dress down as though it is acceptable to be less than formally presented in public. This, it was felt, impresses neither clients nor employees who are both simply bemused.

The reason for all this? In simple terms, business is highly competitive, margins are tight, and results have become the "be all and end all."

All understandable but the view was for leaders to raise the bar of expectation in behaviors at board level, as this would in turn ease the issues within their own teams. Good behaviors are the basis of success and the foundation of trust. There is little point complaining about why people are disengaged when leaders themselves are not adapting to the pressures of the modern environment.

It was noted that the behaviors of many leaders of yesteryear were hardly often of a high level, but the difference was it was another era and far less transparent.

How could this all be changed? The answer:

- Genuine, authentic behaviors
- Leaders who understand the essence of hospitality—trust, integrity, care, compassion, empathy, an understanding of an experience
- Visible, open, and approachable leadership
- The ability to play a real role within communities and socially
- Strong social skills that really do inspire others
- Genuine values and conviction in leadership
- A real understanding of diversity and inclusion—not just lip service
- The ability to walk the talk

Whether one agrees with the aforementioned or not, we are living in a new era, one that does have greater demands that need to be met. There is very little point complaining about people issues if one does not start by reviewing behaviors at the top. This new era has created a new set of pressures and demands that have clearly made many leaders, and moreover their teams, feel stressed, insecure, and vulnerable. It is a logical argument that the existing processes at senior level are either not strong enough or in need for change.

Many companies have voiced their concerns over falling productivity, and yet, this will naturally evolve from trust and the feeling safe and able to even fail?

The Need to Fail

Sports players will often talk about the importance of failure in their learning. It is only through failure that one can learn to succeed. However, there is no doubt that there is a greater fear of failure in business today, both among leaders and employees, which is arguably hindering the development of talent emerging into leadership roles.

The 2019 Vitality report (82) into the healthiest companies noted that:

Productivity and Engagement

- Overall, the results suggest that the employees who took part in the survey lost 14.6 percent of their working hours due to absence (1.1 percent) and presentism (13.4 percent).
- This represents a loss of 38 productive days per employee per year.
- Lost productive time has increased steadily since 2014, when employees were losing 23 days.
- Productivity loss is higher among lower-income workers and younger workers.
- 16.5 percent of employees showed high work engagement levels, an increase from 12.7 percent last year.

Mental Health

- Lower-income employees are the most at-risk for mental health issues, with 16.4 percent of those earning less than 20,000 pounds, indicating that they suffer from depression.
- For the 20,000–30,000-pound income category, the risk remains high at 10.4 percent.
- 56.4 percent of the surveyed employees suffer from at least one dimension of work-related stress.
- 35.1 percent of the employees reported having felt unwell as a consequence of work-related stress.

- Financial concerns are very common, with 51.1 percent of the employees reporting at least some level of concern.
- Employees who have financial concerns are losing more than twice as much productive time than those without and report on significantly unhealthier lifestyle choices.

Lifestyle and Physical Health

- 35.1 percent of the employees say that they sleep less than seven hours per night, and approximately 42 percent have problems with the quality of their sleep.
- Younger employees tend to sleep more hours per night, but are more likely to report problems with the quality of their sleep.
- Younger employees are less likely to eat the recommended five portions of fruit and vegetables per day and are more likely to binge drink or to smoke.
- More than half of the employees' report suffering from two or more musculoskeletal conditions.
- 39.4 percent of the respondents have at least one chronic condition.

Women in the Workplace

- Women report healthier diets, less drinking, and less smoking than men.
- Less likely to exercise enough.
- More likely to suffer from depression.
- More likely to demonstrate high work engagement.

For an advanced economy, the aforementioned is not a strong picture, and it is one that does suggest the need for change. From the preceding analysis, one can begin to understand the underlying stresses that are creating the fear of failure. It is a problem, as it has been demonstrated throughout history, we do need the young to be confident and dynamic. If they begin to feel fearful, then society and business are failing them, and it is at a potentially great cost. There is a real need for talent, as well as for society at large to appreciate that failure, although painful, is an important part of learning, growing, and being successful.

However, the transparency of the modern world makes many believe that failure is a sign of weakness and even see it as a vulnerability in character. It has always been the way, and it will not change. All these views are, in truth, more reflective of those who think them than those that fail. It is one of the reasons why we so often bring sports players to talk and coach industry professionals, as time and again, they will talk of how failure molded them and was the catalyst to their future success.

Failure alone is not a test of character; it is how one responds to failure. To have failed, one must at least have taken a chance and risk, and this is much needed in the modern world.

Sports players will talk about how they embrace failure, as it shows them first-hand how they need to work hard to be able to improve their approach.

This is a complex issue as we all know that the young of today are perhaps less mentally robust as previous generations due to the fact that they have grown up in a safer and less threatening era. However, we also know that they are bright, have great ideas, and a real vision of the future. They need to be encouraged to try and make sure these qualities count. We know that many boards are frustrated with the lack of young leaders breaking through and a lack of those who possess the courage to be risk takers within corporate environments. We need the young to be enabled to not be afraid of failure and setbacks, as without this, little gets challenged, or changed.

It is another of the contradictions of this era, as we know that many of the young are disengaged, and yet, do not robustly challenge leadership teams. As a result, leadership teams have continued along the same road that they can see with not a strong enough understanding of how disengaged the young have been.

Failure is a feature of life. Most CEOs will accept that they have failed many times over, but it has been important to their own learning. To see the best of the emerging generations, there is a need to say openly that failure is to be encouraged, that accepting failure may well free up their individual talents, and that alone is important. Failure is nothing to be concerned about. Not failing is a far bigger concern.

In simplistic terms, the work environment has become an environment that is not a strong nurturing environment for talent, and there is a need for genuine change that is in line with the modern pressures.

Dean Kennett, founder of Fooditude, commented in response to an article that EP published:

'When fear came knocking, it was courage that answered'— something I remind myself and others at times of peril.

It is a mark of the qualities that separate entrepreneurs such as Dean Kennett. They do stand out from those in the corporate world. He launched his business in the mid-2000s, nearly falling during the 2008 crash, as his main client had been an Icelandic bank. He adapted, faced the worst, and came through to build a great new business. However, in the corporate world, this is rare to be seen, but arguably is more needed.

It has become a well-known saying that compares corporates to be like oil tankers, very difficult to turn with any speed. The saying highlights the fact that internal processes become a major internal barrier. A former CEO of ASDA, Allan Leighton, would often talk about the Business Prevention Squads that exist within all businesses, those people whose role it seems to be to stop positive actions and behaviors out of a fear of change. However, this mindset once in the DNA of a company does make it harder to generate positive actions. Those who are trying to take action will feel almost that they will be undermined and vulnerable for trying to do so. The message needs to come from leaders. Allan Leighton spoke the term publicly for good reason; he knew that it highlighted those who possessed negative behaviors and gave them the space to create change. Negativity and process often slow positive behaviors and will naturally create tension and stress.

Stress and Mental Health in the Workplace

Over the last few years, there has been an increased awareness of mental health issues at work, and more is beginning to happen within companies to focus on how the negative dynamics can be changed. One such issue that is often overlooked is anxiety. Research in Australia (84), a country maybe not viewed as being one of high stress, noted that it affects close to 73 percent of the employees in one form or another. A report in the United Kingdom noted 80 percent feel a level of burn out (85). In America, the figure is similar (86). This is a global issue and one that does ask the hard question as to whether change is needed in work across all cultures?

> The world is not doing enough about mental health problems. The stress on younger people is immense. Expectations are bigger. I don't accept that mental health issues have been addressed properly in the Industry. There is a need for people to be more compassionate about this.
>
> There is a general lack of understanding. Unless someone has suffered then the chances are, they will not understand just how it impacts. People need to be comfortable to talk to their bosses about this and the boss should know how to deal with it.

(Paul Clark, Founder and CEO, Inn Vogue Hotels)

This also ties in with the need for talent to feel safe enough to be able to take risk. Anxiety naturally makes a person play within their comfort zones and not take risks. One of the challenges is how to free up the psychology of talent so that they do feel free, able, and less afraid of failure.

One of the issues that is misunderstood is that anxiety within employees has doubled in the last decade. There is genuine fear and concern over work, performance, and financial stability. Over 45 percent of the employees are concerned about their financial stability. At a time, when standards of living have arguably never been higher, we also have higher level of talent that are being restricted through the pressures of life. The argument is that many feel expendable and just a number within a company. There is not a strong enough company culture or ethos that makes people feel valued and important.

In business terms, this is an own goal. One can argue over return on investment (ROI), but it is all pretty pointless if the culture does not free up people to be at their best. Anxiety can reduce work performance by around 15–20 percent, so how does the ROI question work? How is it relevant, as ROI is hindered through increased anxiety?

There is a fair argument emerging that companies will need to follow the example set by sport and have its own lead player with a focus on culture and people that sits apart from the human resources (HR). However, there is still a way to go for many to understand the topic and implications well enough within most companies to see the true value.

> One does hear that a greater percentage of young people have mental health issues. More knowledge is needed, and leaders will need to stop and listen as for many, it is an area that they do not understand.

(Ron Hilvert, Industry elder)

Another recent survey noted that 56 percent of the surveyed employees (86) say that anxiety affects their job performance, and half report a negative impact on relationships with co-workers and peers. Stress in the workplace can take a toll on the entire business operation.

Here are some other facts to place the issue into context:

- In the United States, anxiety affects 40 million (87).
- A study in the *Journal of Applied Psychology* (87) noted that one of the biggest drivers of work performance is interpersonal relationships. Unfortunately, those experiencing anxiety are more likely to avoid their co-workers, hoping to avoid interpersonal conflicts. As work is a collaborative environment, it is easy to see how workplace anxiety may affect the performance of an entire operation. This means that workplace anxiety is more than just a matter of employee health— it has a direct effect on a company's bottom line.
- Turnover has increased among middle management by 10 percent in the last decade. This alone can equate to anything from 100,000 to 2 million pounds depending on the size of the company. It does place the dull ROI question into perspective.

- Top talent wants to work with those companies that possess cultures that free up people.

Most of the research on anxiety in the workplace comes to the same conclusion: when depression and anxiety are effectively treated, companies can reduce the rate of employee turnover and sick days and can improve employee productivity. Providing effective intervention to your employees can help improve your company image and your bottom line.

There is a need for thinking about new strategies that serve to bring back a focus on people and culture. People do need to feel safe and valued.

A progressive approach to mental health can help businesses attract and retain top talent. Today's workers want more than just sick days and paid time off. They want to know that their employers care about them, both personally and professionally. Creating an emotionally and mentally healthy workplace will keep your current workers engaged in their jobs, as well as make your company a coveted place to work.

We don't yet know how to respond and react. There is a learning to take place. It is important that we do become comfortable with this, but it will take time. People have to have an awareness for themselves first—how much sleep do we need, what diet, and so on. What do you do to care for yourself?

For employers, it is important to build in a flexibility in the approach to enable those people who do suffer and how they can adjust the work environment for them. If leaders are able to share their own vulnerability, it will give licence to people to be able to share their concerns too.

(Kathryn Pretzel Shiels, Consultant and mentor)

Capitalism Reset (89)

Most things in life are about a delicate balance and, of course, the growing belief is that business has lost that balance. The argument is that since the global financial crash, companies have continued to make good profits, but have not reinvested sufficiently back into its structures, people, and development, rather than focused on greater shareholder value.

Business needs profits to be reinvested along long-held principles as well as rewarding shareholders. Without this reinvestment, it is no real surprise that we are seeing many of the problems that we are today with talent opting out, disengagement, cynicism, and a growing lack of trust in business leadership.

We know that emerging generations leave jobs frequently and are seeking to work for those companies that really do carry a social as well as commercial purpose. It is easy to patronize the younger generations and say that is just the way of millennials, but maybe, companies do hold a responsibility?

One knows that the balance has been lost when *The Financial Times* (FT), the City of London's leading voice and paper, launches a campaign in September 2019 called *The New Agenda* or *Capitalism Reset* arguing that:

> In the decade since the global financial crash, the model has come under strain, particularly in focusing on maximising profit and shareholder value. These principles of good business are necessary but not sufficient. It is time for a reset.
>
> The long-term health of free capitalism will depend on delivering profit with purpose. Companies will come to understand that this combination serves their self-interest as well as that of their customers and employees. Without change, the prescriptions risk being far more painful (89).

These are strong words from a newspaper such as the FT and say much. Business is facing new challenges and change. There will be a need for new roles to be created in the boardroom as companies today face the challenges of building trust back with their own people, let alone customers. The lack of trust exists for good and fair reason and patronizing the emerging generations has, at best, been unhelpful. It does need people at the board table that will bring new thinking and that will challenge the board in its actions.

Over the last few years, many discussions about investment in people, in culture, in social enterprises, in innovation have been almost seen as a luxury item. During austerity, one may make the case, but the austerity piece is a bit like Brexit and gets used to cover a wide range of issues. This is as simple as being about core values and principles or pillars that a business stands for and believe in, beyond making profit. That is what employees want to see: businesses that do stand for something greater than self-interest, and the irony is that this is what customers also want to see. There is a reason why the FT led such a campaign, which was a brave move. There is a reason why it is stated that the majority of employees do not trust in their leadership teams.

Business today needs to find its old principles and pillars once again. It does need to think differently and be prepared to reinvest in those things that will build trust back into business and in work environments. This can involve reinvesting in people, in culture, in social enterprises, but most of all, it is about business leaders understanding the issues and creating the change that so many desire.

As the FT campaign indicates, this is not to be seen as a cost, but a way of engaging again with both customers and employees, and in setting leaders free to lead with conviction.

CHAPTER 9

Should Leaders Be Visible?

One of the great criticisms of many business leaders today is that they are not accessible or visible. This, it is argued, has contributed to a natural fall in trust. It does tie very closely into the key issues raised in Chapter 8, creating an environment where one feels both trusted and safe. Is it a fair expectation to see one's leader on the front line? Is it fair to expect them to be both visible and accessible?

The counter-argument is that the workloads placed on all senior executives have increased, giving less time to be visible, and that in hospitality, the most important leadership takes place on the front line. The real leaders are the reception managers, the restaurant managers, the customer services manager. Does it really matter how the chief executive officer (CEO) or managing director (MD) communicates, as the most important leader is the operational lead?

There are many who would support this view.

> Unfortunately leaders are caught up in various aspect of the business today which pulls them away from the traditional role of the Hospitality leader ... in front of guests and teams delivering the service promise. Leaders today are caught up in the finance, commercial aspect and strategic part of the business—which is more often than not consuming 80–90 percent of their days.

(Thomas Sorcinelli, F&B Director, Heckfield Place)

Grant Campbell, the General Manager at the Nobu Hotel, London, noted that:

> You are as visible as you want to be. Yes, admittedly at times it is easy to be absorbed in areas of the role that keeps you away from the operation. It is important that when you do have time with the operation it should be spent in a quality way. Not necessarily

work focused but interactive and social. With the use of technology, you can be very much in the operation even when not physically there. When I am physically there, I will often work within the outlets and ensure that I am seen as available with the team and for the guests.

Underlying the issue is one of managing demands and priorities. For many, they hope that their team is full of leaders who are visible even when the General Manager cannot be. Leadership is a relative constant, but the overall demands have increased alongside increased technology. General Managers are required to be available, almost to the point of constantly, and time-related deliverables come with high expectations. Leaders need to find what works for them and their teams.

It is all about finding the right balance. Any good team will have a number of leaders, but it is always important to understand that responsibility lies with one person only, and it is that person that, regardless of others, teams will look toward for their voice and leadership. It is not something that can ever be delegated. The great sports teams never have just one captain but a number across the field of play.

The other piece that is often overlooked in this part of the debate is that the power of informal communications. It is not always about the words spoken, but the informal communications that can take place between a leader and his or her team. It could be a simple smile, a reassuring hand on the shoulder, a joke to ease the tension, or a simple piece of humanity. It can be the most human aspects of how leaders interact, which develops respect and trust. Many will counter-argue that it has become increasingly difficult to interact informally out of fear of their actions being misinterpreted. However, a balance and confidence in behavior needs to be found.

The Importance of Visibility

Most leaders believe that it is important to be visible.

100% leaders should be more visible. You need to be part of the front line. The emphasis today has moved from service to analysis.

I used to see leaders who excelled in leadership. Now I see leaders who excel in spreadsheets, but spreadsheets do not run a hotel. You have to be out there. We need people who are warm and out there, shaking hands, being human. How proud are you of your business?

(Bill Walshe, CEO, The Viceroy Group)
Michael Gray, a former VP Hyatt in London, agrees:

I feel so strongly about this. General Managers are no longer walking the floor in their hotels: not in the lobbies, not welcoming guests. By not doing this, how can they know when things are not quite right? Leadership is often about a feeling in the air, about instinct and you cannot have that from afar. General Managers have pulled away from what they are good at which is all about the people but one needs to be there with the teams when things are not going right and even when they are. It is people that make hospitality special and we should never forget that.

This is a debate that rages on not just in hospitality, but across many businesses. What is a fair expectation of leadership? It is no coincidence that in the world of politics that leaders do tend to be very visible on a constant basis. Just consider the problems that the Australian Prime Minister faced when he did not turn up on the front line during the crisis with the bush fires at the start of the year. He initially refused to cut his holiday short from Hawaii as the fires raged. He argued that there was little he could do. No one expected the prime minister to place himself on the front line, but they expected him to be present and share their disaster, essentially far better behaviors were expected than they saw. The result was that he did lose control of the situation and most importantly, respect.

Leadership is often about being visible and having the courage to be bigger than a situation; it is about not trying to protect oneself, but to be there for others. This is why, visible leadership is just so important in all leadership.

Vicky La Trobe noted in interview:

You cannot lead if you are not seen. A good leader is all about personality, how they are perceived, how they are connected, how transparent they are, honest and real. They must be seen. There is no excuse for a leader not to be visible to an employee.

There is a very senior industry CEO who has often been described as egocentric with a need to be in the limelight. In truth, this is far from the truth. The private person had no need to be seen, but, rightly or wrongly, he believed that it was his job as leader to be seen at the major events.

When attending an event where there was a speaker, he would purposefully delay his entrance to close to when the audience was all sitting down so that they would all see him walk to the front and introduce himself to the speaker. He would then always be the second person to ask a question from the audience. He simply saw this as part of his job. In fairness, it is hard to argue against it, as his business results have long been of the highest level. He attracted criticism and attracted some of the best talent in equal measure.

Another important example is that of the BP CEO, Tony Hayward, at the time of oil spill in the Gulf of Mexico. One of his first reactions was to try to shift blame away from BP.

In an interview with the BBC, the chief executive Tony Hayward attempted to shift the blame for the accident to the U.S. owner of the sunken rig, Transocean, which was at the center of the spill. "This was not our accident … This was not our drilling rig … This was Transocean's rig. Their systems. Their people. Their equipment" (90).

The statement was made before any real investigations had taken place, and it displayed a desire to place self-protection above the genuine tragedy taking place. Later, he would comment, when asked about the amount of oil and dispersant flowing into the gulf, he responded:

The Gulf of Mexico is a very big ocean. The amount of volume of oil and dispersant we are putting into it is tiny in relation to the total water volume.

While technically correct, the comments made the company appear aloof and unconcerned about the environmental damage being done. This was then followed up with a very public photograph of Hayward sailing in the Solent with his son on a Sunday morning. In fairness, it was his weekend, but it displayed a leader that seemed not to care enough about the responsibilities of his company to the environment. He soon lost his role.

Leadership is about inspiring confidence in others and being there when things do go wrong, which is why the debate over visibility is so important.

In the United States and United Kingdom, this is of prime importance, as leaders play such important roles beyond the day to day. It is why leadership is such an important subject matter.

> In my opinion, you cannot be truly successful unless you are visible in your business, to your team, to the owner and to the business community.

(Ronen Nissenbaum, President and CEO Dan Hotels)

There are numerous case studies that show that those companies that possess highly visible leaders perform well and often attract the best talent. It does breed confidence within teams who, rightly or wrongly, see a leader as standing with them and being on the front line of the business.

> 100%, leaders need to be more visible. You need to be part of the front line. Leaders have an obligation to communicate a purpose to their teams. Our ideology is based around making people proud and from that, we believe in a "pride before profit" culture in leadership.

(Chris Franzen, Area VP Western India for Hyatt)

The question is how visible is visible? Does one need to be simply visible to one's teams or to a wider audience?

Of course, the answer will vary. In politics, the leader needs to be visible as their responsibility is to the voter, and they need to speak directly to that audience. Both the election successes of President Obama and President Trump have been linked to their use of social media and how they both bypassed the traditional mediums to talk directly to the electorates. In business, of course, the situation is different, and arguably, visibility is more important to the internal teams than to an external audience.

Russell Kett, Chairman of HVS, commented:

> All good teams need a number of leaders and if you are the General Manager or the CEO, you need to bring the best out of these people. You need to respect and listen to each other; you need to have an environment where people are aware how they are as individuals and how they fit into the whole picture. Being visible has two aspects to it: Are you visible to the guest or are you visible to your team?
>
> You cannot lead a team if you are an invisible person but if you are sitting in an office, you need to have a good person interacting with the guests that will give them the confidence of being welcomed and control. Nowadays, business does require people to spend more time on paperwork but that is only one part of the job. A leader's role is to create an environment that everybody, whether guests or staff, feel comfortable in. In that environment you do need to be visible, most especially when things do go wrong.

Mark Pitcher, a leading Industry podcaster with Smash the Box (91), offers a broader perspective:

> In Hospitality, leadership should be visible, but leadership should start with creating intent. You can be invisible and still do the right things. There is a myth about the need for extrovert leaders because there are many introverts who are very good and able. This is where technology can play an important role because there is no reason not to be seen today. You can use video, hologram messaging, bring in your personality and find ways to communicate effectively.

I personally believe in management by walking around—but to do this well, starts with self-awareness. One needs to be genuine and honest—not trying to be someone else. That is my starting intention, to let people know that I am there for them; that you have their back and that you have their best interests at heart. If I can live and breathe that, then the chances are all will be ok.

The question for all leaders is—do your people feel that they belong? If so, then something is working well.

Mark raises an interesting question—can a leader be an introvert, and if so, can they be an effective leader?

I am naturally extrovert, but it is not a question of whether someone is an extrovert or an introvert—the question is whether the team trusts in them? I have known many good leaders that have operated with the minimum amount of noise—just a simple word to the right person. It is about the person's ability to lead. If you are in Hospitality, you generally have a love for people so most want to be visible.

(Adam Elliott, Founder, Paragon Hospitality)

CHAPTER 10

Attracting the Best Talent: Nurturing of the Young

If any Industry wants to have strong leaders, then it does need to be able to attract the best talent and nurture it effectively. In the field of hospitality, this has always been a major area of debate, as the industry is a relatively unique mix of major skills sets that include a need for strong business acumen, the ability to lead teams that are multi-disciplined, and include the creative and craft based, being able to socialize with both Heads of State and the average man on the street, and finally, the ability, to create safe havens for guests to have an experience of one level or another.

All this does lead immediately to a number of key areas of debate:

- Does a leader need to be a graduate? Should they be able to work their way up from the bottom if they have the skills?
- The industry is changing so fast; is it fair to expect hotel schools and universities to be aligned to the needs of industry? Are they, and if not, what needs to happen?
- Is the industry competitive in both attracting the best talent and in selling its own story as a career?
- Is the industry truly nurturing the leaders of tomorrow?

Once again, there are few black and white answers, but it is a key area for discussion. Debate on the preceding questions has raged on for many years, and in fairness, there has been no lack of investment. However, progress does need to be made as the industry today is world class, and it is mildly ridiculous if the industry is not selling itself well enough and does not have a strong enough support system that is nurturing talent.

So, where do we stand?

Education

Has the Education System Been Good Enough in Supporting the Development of New Leaders?

This is an understandably controversial area for discussion, but if one discusses the lack of emerging leaders breaking through, then it is also important to cast an eye toward the system that is nurturing this talent. Has it been effective enough?

There are international and regional differences, but regardless, the hard question is: are many hotel and business schools fit for purpose and good enough?

The development of talent in higher education should ideally be a marriage between businesses and education working closely together. Is it fair to ask if this has been good enough? The previous chapters have high-lighted the issues and changes taking place within business, so it is only right that the same questions be posed in relation to education.

One of the core arguments for why emerging talent has not broken through into leadership positions as early as in previous eras is that all business today carries a higher level of risk. Margins are often tighter. There is greater demand from shareholders. The world is far more trans-parent and open, every mistake is maximized, and there has been an increasing move toward the use of legal action on mistakes. At the same time, the disciplines and knowledge needed in leadership are growing.

Business is, therefore, cautious and concerned over any risk profile. So, the question is, can the young be better prepared for the challenge ahead? As the concern over risk has grown, has the preparation of talent adapted accordingly? There is a need for young talent to be nurtured into leadership roles.

There are undoubtedly some leading hotel schools all across the world, including the likes of the great Swiss hotel schools such as Ecole Hoteliere de Lausanne, Les Roches, Glion, the Cesar Ritz School, to The Hague and Cornell, but are they enough? Is the system strong enough?

Hospitality Skills Are a Premium

It has long been an area of debate that many believe that hospitality is not viewed as a genuine profession nor leading skill set in its own right. However, many outside the industry have a far more appreciative and respectful attitude toward the importance or premium value of hospitality skill sets. One argument maybe that the industry needs to do more to engage with the leading schools, as there are businesses from across all sectors that happily and actively recruit from hospitality schools.

Hospitality is a business that not only excites interest, it has skilled world-class practitioners who have a much-desired skill set. Business sectors, including banking, legal to financial services, like to recruit from hospitality skills. They do not view hospitality schools as the poor relation to many management and business schools. A true hospitality skill set is of such importance and should be valued more highly.

The industry is world class, and it does need the strong structure of hotel schools that can support it well. Not just any hotel school, but one that is truly progressive, in tune with the young, with industry, and that can really help nurture younger talent. The Swiss hotel schools have led the way, and they have developed a well-deserved reputation for excellence. There is, however, a need for more all across the world. The business environment today is becoming increasingly more complex, and there is a need to ensure that, in order to prepare and nurture good leaders of tomorrow, this learning is in place. Regardless of whether one agrees with the aforementioned or not, the truth is that hospitality is one of the leading global industries that does impact on economies all across the world and does needs a strong support framework that nurtures young talent.

The industry should be striving to create centers of excellence in the key disciplines to really engage and develop the skills of the young. It does need to make a stronger argument for itself. It needs to be going into schools, making sure that the young are trained not just in cooking, but in their social skills. Strong social competence and the ability to be a visible leader are two of the most important skills in life, regardless of the industry.

Those who are generally drawn into hospitality possess a desire to be close to environments that are vibrant, positive, and that offer service and care for others. The very essence of a hospitality skill set starts with a desire to *give to others*, to interact socially and to like people. Hospitality is not just about learning business skills; it is also about the social and craft. It is multidimensional and needs strong programs. It also needs a strong alliance between industry and education.

What are the core issues?

Based to commentary from industry, these seem to be broken down into a number of core areas:

- The industry does not *sell* itself as well as is possible to the young, highlighting that it is an excellent profession and progressive in its approach.
- Too many focus on management skills over craft.
- Many graduates emerge with unrealistic expectations.

Ron Hilvert, one of the founding forces in the rise of Jumeirah and of the Emirates Academy, noted that:

> There are a number of areas where improvement is needed. There are not enough world class Hospitality programmes. There is a lack of quality teaching and simply, a lot of the schools are not good enough in Hospitality. There needs to be an overall step up with better practical education and a need to provide the knowledge relevant today of the operating issues in business.

Marc Dardenne, Accor, would tend to agree:

> The Hospitality schools have not been in tune with what is happening in the world. They could do a better job by being closer to the reality.

Bill Washe, CEO of the Viceroy Group, would agree:

> Relying on the old curriculum is no longer sufficient. On the World Economic Forum, a survey of the top skills and workforce strategies noted the following list:

1. Complex problem-solving
2. Critical thinking
3. Creativity
4. People management
5. Coordinating with others
6. Emotional intelligence
7. Decision-making
8. Service orientation
9. Negotiation
10. Cognitive flexibility

How are many of these being taught? We are living in a faster society, we want people to be able to make immediate decisions and have the ability to solve problems in a much faster pace.

Twenty years ag.o, the education in Hospitality was different. You would spend half a year in business and half the year in school. Now they have a four-year college term and when they finish, they come on the job not knowing anything about the reality. I think a return to real experience would be more beneficial.

The challenge is adapting education at the same pace that industry is changing. Is it natural that the educational system is lagging behind change? Is there a need for schools to change the way that they think about the knowledge they need to bring into learning?
Ronen Nissenbaum, President and CEO of Dan Hotels, noted that:

The education system has evolved and continues to do so. Most graduates are prepared with a theoretical knowledge but more on the job, practical training is needed to be incorporated into the curriculum. It is essential that the students experience real life work environments to ascertain the fit to the Industry.

Marco Nijhof, Group Director of Hospitality for Value Retail, went a step further:

Certain schools are too focused on the hotelier's side of the business but there needs to be more focus on the owner side of the business—a greater understanding needs to be created so that a link with the hotelier side of the business can be taught and understood—real estate, asset management, reasons for ownership, and so on.

Many of the industry experts interviewed did question whether the system has been fit for purpose and if it is in need of evolution? Most will accept that there is great talent in the system. The question is not about this but about the overall structure.

Vicky La Trobe (consultant) commented that:

We have been training people in the same way for a long period of time and it does not suit everybody. There are a lot of people who cannot thrive within a structured education system. The technical side of education has declined but these skills are fundamental so one has to ask if the system is fit for purpose?

Hospitality is a very different industry in that we have had many leaders who have worked their way up from the bottom. This has become less so as more and more institutional investors have become involved and they want to see leading qualifications but there does need to be a strong balance between management studies and the technical.

But, the issues are broader:

Michael Gray, former VP with Hyatt, commented on the need of hospitality to be far more engaging.

If we want the best young leaders, then the Industry needs to compete for them. We need to encourage people to come to work in Hospitality. We are way down there on the list in the eyes of the parents, career officers, and teachers. They don't think about our Industry seriously. The pay level is part of the issue, but this has improved a lot in recent years. We need more people talking about the Industry for what it is—a great Industry where you can have a wonderful career, an enjoyable career. We need to encourage school children and engage them proactively.

Russell Kett, Chairman of HVS, agrees:

> If we really want to deal with this properly, we should have started to educate school children about hotels and the hospitality business from an extremely young age. We should expose primary school children to what the Industry can offer . . . part of the problem has been that many equate Hospitality to being servile and this is not a natural thing for anyone to want to be. That is because we have sold it badly. The hotel schools have had to evolve to not just producing people who can cook but also be business orientated. The business management side of schools does need to improve. There are great schools out there turning out good people but there needs to be more.

There are so many that do argue that hospitality is an industry where the personal traits and strengths are more important than a degree qualification.

> I do think that while there are many strong Hospitality programmes, the Hospitality Industry is comprised of a diverse set of backgrounds that aren't necessarily reliant on a degree in the Industry or formal Hospitality training via the education system. I believe that you should hire for attitude and train for skills—you want someone who is a natural fit for the Hospitality Industry coupled with passion and a drive and determination to learn the skills needed.

(Martin Rinck, Chief Brand Officer, Hilton in Vancouver)
It is fair to say that there is work to be done.

CHAPTER 11

The Power of Networking

Networking is a necessity in our business as it can serve to not only open doors, but build knowledge and build new important relationships.

(Martin Jones, VP with Starwood)

Many believe that the skill and ability to network effectively is one of the defining differences between the baby boomer generations and the millennials. It is natural enough as the baby boomers grew up in an age pre the Internet and e-mail; networking, therefore was of increased social and business importance. The millennials and Generation Z have lived in a work environment where there have always been e-mails, mobile phones, and the Internet.

Yes, social interaction skills have, I believe declined from our generation's perspective. However, I would argue that the emerging generation are more socially engaged than we have been but they engage through technology.

(Chris Franzen, VP Hyatt for Western India)

"Captaincy is 90% luck and 10% skill but don't do it without the 10%" (92)

The above was a tongue-in-cheek quote from a legendary former Australian cricket captain, Richie Benaud. In truth, the balance is probably closer to 40–60, as one needs luck with the people one has in a team, and the 100 uncontrollable factors that come into play. It was Napoleon who noted that he wanted generals who were *lucky*. The margins of success can be very fine. Is the luck needed defined by age and experience, or is it that the relationships that one possesses can make all the difference? It is a well-known old saying that success comes "from not what you know but who you know." Life has not changed all that much since whenever that comment was first uttered. No one knows the true source, but there was a report this year that noted that 66 percent of Brits still believed it held true (93).

If one can enhance one's opportunities through relationships, then, of course, it would be nonsensical not to work hard to build more of them. Leadership can be a very lonely place at the worst of times, and relationships can make all the difference. Networking and building relationships are vitally important skill sets to possess.

It was Tony Blair who noted that he became increasingly unpopular, the better and more competent a prime minister that he became. It is often noted that many leaders become increasingly cynical and defensive with time and age, as leadership takes its toll. It often needs the confidence of the young to inspire, but it is a trait that is said to be becoming increasingly rare to find in the young. Is this true, or do leaders today need to do more to encourage the young to lead?

So much of business today is about risk management, and young leaders are seen to be a risk, so a more defensive approach is often taken—but does this then potentially erode something of real value?

Is it a coincidence that the two leading candidates for the 2020 U.S. Presidential Elections are aged over 70?

If one goes further, of the leading democrats who ran:

- Joe Biden—77 years old
- Bernie Saunders—78 years old
- Elizabeth Warren—70 years old
- Michael Bloomberg—78 years old

This is a long way from the days of Bill Clinton becoming President when he was 46 years old, JFK was 43. Barrack Obama was 47. Abraham Lincoln was 52.

Many would argue that the world was a safer place under the younger presidents, so why has there been such a shift toward experience and age over allowing youth its opportunity?

Moreover, Bloomberg started his own business in 1981, aged 39. Trump started in his family's business, aged 15, and Bernie Sanders was the Mayor of Burlington in Vermont, aged 39. Where along the road did business lose trust in giving young leaders the opportunity?

Maybe there is a need once again to place trust in talent rather than experience?

How does this all relate to the importance of networking? Part of building trust and confidence is by being visible and accessible to audiences. Networking is a key part of building confidence and ensuring that relationships are in place. It does tie back into the chapter on visibility, but it is also important to have a focus on building strong relationships all across a market. In simplistic terms, it is currency, not money, but the ability to access knowledge, support, help, and open doors when it matters.

Both the British and Americans have always traditionally loved their leaders and captains. They hold special places in the eyes of many, but there has been a gradual erosion in how leaders have been viewed, and there is less and less spoken today about leadership and more about structures, models, and process, both in sport and in business. Thirty years ago, most chief executive officers (CEOs) within a sector were almost revered and household names. Today, research tells us that most aspiring young managers can name less than four leaders in their discipline.

There is no questioning that business today is more professional, but it was arguably more fun and open 20 years ago when leaders were more visible. It is also true that leadership can be a fickle friend, as one often goes from hero to villain at a speed based on a factor beyond the leader. Regardless, leadership is still so important to the psyche and important to a group. Peoples, from all across the globe, are traditionally tribal and continue to want to belong to a group.

The perception of the British may be one of politeness and restraint, but it is far from the truth. The Brits are as passionate a race as exists, and they follow people, so it is essential that leadership is encouraged as an important skill. It can be devalued by models and process, as it does determine perhaps not the overall output, but definitely the psychology of a group. It impacts directly on the confidence of a business.

One only has to look at the market leading businesses within a sector or the most admired, and one will see visible leaders; leaders who do communicate.

In these most challenging of times, we surely would like to see leaders who are out there, clear, visible, and accessible as this builds confidence. One may not agree with them, but it does also build behaviors. Its builds strength in others.

So, perhaps leadership is 33 percent luck, 33 percent how it makes other people respond, and 33 percent skill? Whatever the truth, it is important to nurture in the young; give them the same chances that many previously, good or bad, were given in the past, for it did not turn out too badly.

The Negative Myth Surrounding Networking

It is clear that there needs to be a new emphasis placed on building relationships that are real and have genuine meaning. Networking was an important traditional skill that has been eroded by both social media and a negative perspective linked to the concept.

Many have come to almost dislike the thought of networking, as they view it as something that is almost inauthentic, and there is an element of truth in this, as in days gone by, networking could often be exactly this. The pet hate of many is the person who looks at your name badge to decide whether you are worthy of time, or looks over your shoulder while talking to you to see if there is someone else for them to target while *working the room*.

It can be the home of the inauthentic, but that is not true networking. We get the superficial in all walks and parts of life. That is not networking, that is poor behaviors.

Real networking, skilled networking is about the opposite, treating people with care and interest, acting with good behaviors. Without being sexist in anyway, one of the real missing skill sets of recent years has been the wives of leaders who back in the 1950s, 1960s, and 1970s knew how to host social events and were highly skilled in creating social frameworks for networking.

This is partly because of how the society has changed. In the days of the 1950s, 1960s, and 1970s, most wives did not work and were focused on supporting their husbands. Today, often, both partners work and have full days. Their only time for socializing is either with close family friends who accept the children being awake or after children's bedtimes. It is naturally limiting. However, it has been an important *event* lost while many parents today complain of feeling isolated.

Sociologists have been writing on this issue, as many parents are investing more time into their children and feel too pressurized to cook, so simply withdraw. It is argued that the number of people hosting dinner parties has fallen by over 50 percent in the 30 years from the late 1970s to early 2000s (94).

This is all understandable, but our own findings are that many want to see a change in this trend. We have a desire for more real-time conversations with colleagues and friends. The old-fashioned concept of the *French farmers table*, which brings groups together to dine together, is growing in both desire and importance. In our own research (EP Business in Hospitality), we find that over 60 percent want to spend more time in informal and safe social situations that are not work-focused, but have a focus on *life*. The move is toward a desire to network and socialize, but in environments where there are like-minded individuals and no pretense.

Pretense is maybe the heart of the change. The parties of the 1950s, 1960s, and 1970s were full of pretense, and they became a negative. Today, many want to socialize, but it must be something that offers a real connection, a shared hobby or joy, and all with an air of informality. In today's world, there is a mistrust of anything not genuine, so the skill is to be both genuine and authentic. It is about engaging people with a desire to learn, to pick up new knowledge.

It was often said that the best way to get someone to like them is to get them to talk about themselves. There is truth in this too, but the real skill is to have an interest in them. The starting place of networking is having a desire to learn. Networking allows the opportunity to build new friendships, to gain new information, to have real conversations that allow me to learn.

Perhaps, this is the heart of the issue: somewhere along the road, we forgot that building real conversation with strangers and actually having care about new people is a good thing. In the last 20 years, people network less. They have less conversation, but they spend more time building online social connections that mean so very little in the real world. So many boast about how many social connections they have. It appears on hundreds of CVs as though everyone should be impressed, but, in truth, the key is to do the opposite.

Is it a coincidence that there is a concern that many possess less knowledge, are narrower in their thinking at the same time as conversation has fallen as has networking? I suspect not.

There will be a hundred research reports that will say that networking is important, that it builds business connections and trust. So, do try to look at the issue through a new perspective, as it is essential. Moreover, it says something good about you.

Network to learn. Network to build knowledge. Network to find new friendships. Now, why do people view networking negatively?

CHAPTER 12

The Dyslexia Myth—the Catalyst for Many Leaders

Dyslexics have long faced jokes over their disability, such as "Scrabble was invented by Nazis to piss off kids with dyslexia" (Eddie Izzard) (95). All well intentional, but dyslexia has been seen for many years as a weakness, when, in truth, it has been a major strength. For hospitality, it has been the source of great talent. Many of the great general managers and chefs have been dyslexia sufferers. If one reads the roll call of those who suffered from dyslexia, then one soon realizes how any negative perspective was foolish.

"Children with disabilities are stronger than we know, they fight the battles that most will never know (96)." —**Misti Renea Neely**

It may seem strange that a book on leadership is writing about the link between dyslexia and leadership until one surveys the list of those who have been sufferers over the years. It is clear that there must be qualities within dyslexics that do act as catalysts to many becoming influential leadership figures.

Firstly, a list of some of America's leading political figures who have been seen as dyslexic include:

- George Washington
- Andrew Jackson
- Woodrow Wilson
- Nelson Rockefeller

If one then turns one's eyes toward business legends, there are:

- Sir Richard Branson
- Henry Ford
- Ted Turner
- Lord Sugar
- Jamie Oliver
- Anita Roddick

Actors and actresses such as:

- Jennifer Anniston
- Danny Glover
- Oliver Reed
- Jay Leni
- Keanu Reeves
- Billy Bob Thornton
- Loretta Young
- Orlando Bloom

Sports figures such as:

- Sir Steve Redgrave
- Caitlyn Jenner
- Sir Jackie Stewart
- Muhammed Ali

Even Albert Einstein and Stephen Spielberg.

It is fair to say that we can learn from the aforementioned. In hospitality, there have been many great chefs and hoteliers who have been dyslexic.

Dean Kennett, Founder of the Food Service company, Fooditude, commented:

Having suffered in my younger years and still to this day, I have to check three times or more before sending something. Things have changed now but I can remember getting singled out and made fun of, this in turn stops you from putting your hand up to answer and the effects are long lasting in life. I still get the odd poke from someone that I've misspelled or put down bad grammar in a paragraph. To me it sounds right, to others it obviously doesn't. It did inhibit me for years to write what I was expressing and this in turn increases your inability to express yourself effectively and with gusto. What I've learnt is to build up my resilience and when someone points something out, just thank them and move on. But through it all, I believe I found my own way to do things, set a different pattern and ultimately never conformed to the party line.

Dyslexia is not the terrible foe in learning maybe, as it was once viewed. Some dyslexics will argue that it helped them to have more compassion toward others as they were made to feel as though they were a failure in school, and that they had to work twice as hard in order to make any progression. Others will note that although their dyslexia was a barrier to learning, it accentuated their more creative skills.

Interestingly, there is a very strong link between dyslexia and entrepreneurship, which maybe a natural result of many feeling as though they were different, even an outsider while at school.

An interesting article was published on the subject in 2011. The article posed the question as to whether dyslexics had vision that others did not possess? It also noted that 80 percent of the people viewed dyslexia as a form of being retarded even as recently as this last decade (97).

They're in good company. Richard Branson, Charles Schwab, Ted Turner, and Cisco CEO John Chambers are all dyslexic. Even Henry Ford had the disorder. . . . They come to the realisation that society pronounces the number of skill sets that are necessary for success that they don't seem to have. And they go out and build the environment in which they will impact. That's sort of my working hypothesis to explain why all these entrepreneurs exist who have traits of dyslexia.

The correlation between dyslexia and entrepreneurship has long been a subject of scientific inquiry. In 2004, the Cass Business School (98) in London found that 20 percent of the English entrepreneurs polled said they were dyslexic, while managers "reflected the UK national dyslexia incidence level of 4 percent." In the United States, however, the results were even more persuasive: the same researchers behind the UK study found that 35 percent of the American entrepreneurs surveyed identified themselves as dyslexic.

It has been well documented that people who have dyslexia are good at problem solving and focusing on the wider picture combined with a strong work ethic and a high level of compassion. In leadership, these skills are often of absolute importance.

In the United Kingdom, one of the hospitality industry's leading entrepreneurs in food service, William Baxter, was dyslexic. One of the features that distinguished William from others was the fact that he always had time for people and very rarely, beyond his office walls, have a bad word to say about anyone. Another leading figure of the industry who also suffered is Peter Lederer CBE who oversaw the growth to success of Gleneagles during the 1990s. The best testament to the success of Peter Lederer in Scotland is the fact that the Scottish industry has viewed him as one of their own and their leader in hospitality for over the last 30 years. Lederer's skill was to listen expertly and be able to change the course of meetings with his input. Always calm, always measured, one would ever know that he has struggled.

It is said that many dyslexics are driven through learning from the failures they feel during the school years. There is little doubt that the educational system took time to understand the issues thrown up by dyslexics. Therefore, there are many who feel they have a point to prove in their career, that they are not failures, and their motivation is arguably higher than that of many.

There will be story after story of many who failed exams in their school days and adapted by working hard on practical life skills in order to progress and find another road forward. If one was to create a stereotypical story, it would be of a young person who struggled through school and "couldn't wait for it to end." In their teens, they had already shown evidence of an entrepreneurial spirit, washing neighbors' cars and cutting grass. They were always going to find it difficult to find a job, so either resorted to a job that had a focus on either craft skills, such as carpentry, cookery, or on social skills such as sales where they would spend time with people and not on administration. From this, they would find a new business idea that they would create and build.

Research does suggest that dyslexics are disproportionately represented among entrepreneurs. It is suggested that that 20 percent of the UK's business self-starters have the condition. The U.S. market showed that 35 percent of company founders identified themselves as dyslexic, compared with 15 percent in the general population.

A research report, compiled by Julie Logan, Professor of Entrepreneurship at Cass University in 2015 (98), noted that:

> The Industry is one to which dyslexics are drawn to as they can get around their weaknesses in reading and writing and play to their strengths. . . . One reason that dyslexics are drawn to entrepreneurship . . . is that strategies they have used since childhood to offset their weaknesses in written communication and organisational ability—identifying trustworthy people and handing over major responsibilities to them—can be applied to businesses.

For hospitality, those suffering from dyslexia has long been known to be a great source of talent. One of the many concerns that does get raised regarding the relatively recent dominance of job boards in recruitment is whether it has served to create another barrier for dyslexics to overcome. Is there a danger that the industry has been *pushing away* this talent pool?

The simple answer is dyslexics will find a way through regardless, but certainly, the industry needs to be thoughtful and considered in this area, as dyslexics have long played an important and constructive role in hospitality, let alone all industries. It will be foolhardy not to encourage talent that understands social skills, compassion, oral skills, and hard work ethic.

PART IV

What Does the Past Tell Us?

CHAPTER 13

What Does History Tell Us Is Important About Leadership?

It is said that hospitality businesses are better managed today, but is this true? Has the industry changed as much as many will argue that it has? The hospitality story over the last century has been one of real growth and success. In that time, it has become a truly global industry, with a number of household names that most can easily name. There must, therefore, be good reason in how this was achieved and what drove these businesses to grow so successfully?

There are many that argue that the industry today has become too reliant on brands and become less innovative, with less loyalty, and with fewer new leaders breaking through. They argue that business processes may be better today, but often, it is also more rigid and less inventive in its approach to breaking new ground.

Where Does the Truth Lie?

The hospitality industry has a long and proud heritage in great leaders who have paved the path over the many years to be the world-class industry that it is today. This includes many great hoteliers, visionaries, chefs, and strong business characters that have built the industry from all across the globe. This includes the likes of Cesar Ritz (99) and Richard D'Oyly Carte (100) through to Lord Forte (101) to Conrad Hilton (102), J. Williard Marriott (103) to the immense influence of the French with the likes of the great chef, Paul Bocuse (104) to the founder of the global enterprise Sodexo, Pierre Bellon (105). These are just some of the legends who built the industry we see today. They also paved the way for hospitality to be a truly international business, one where anyone can build a career, travel the world, and find new experiences.

All the above figures were very different people, but all understood the importance of both innovating, having good and loyal people. It is something that has arguably been lost in recent times, as there has been a growing pre-occupation with business models, processes, and systems over innovation and people. All these leading figures from the past built exceptional businesses in the markets and economies of their time. Some may argue that they were less competitive times, less demanding eras, but the bottom line is that they succeeded and exceled in their own time, and that they became legends of the industry. Business has not changed all that dramatically over the years, although as the previous chapter noted, the focus and emphasis of business's priorities have changed. Does this mean that business is better today, or that leaders are better? There are always lessons to be learned from the past, and so, it is important to be aware of the legacy inherited and how it was built.

It is said that businesses do evolve and grow through cycles, and maybe it is time for another stage in evolution or perhaps even a return to values and principles that have worked in the past.

As we write for the future, it is of course also correct that we acknowledge the past as the two are closely linked.

The Shift Back to the Past

If one looks back at the history of the industry, a number of core themes do emerge being simply a genuine passion for hospitality and service over business models. This was arguably the major shift that has taken place in recent years, but does this mean that hospitality businesses are better today?

Some would argue on both sides of this discussion. It is, however, important to understand the founding principles of the key leaders and figures that helped build the industry.

J. Willard Marriott

If one takes the example of J. Willard Marriott, even after the company grew to include hundreds of restaurants and hotels, Marriott was still very involved directly in the business. He vowed to personally inspect every establishment at least four times a year. He was also known to be highly devoted to his employees. According to his son, Bill—"In establishing the culture of the company, there was a lot of attention and tender loving care paid to the hourly workers. When they were sick, he went to see them. When they were in trouble, he got them out of trouble. He created a family loyalty" (106). As Marriott himself commented, "You've got to make your employees happy. If the employees are happy, they are going to make the customers happy" (107).

It is one of the contradictions of the discussion regarding business models, as arguably, life today is the safest that it has ever been—bar the coronavirus crisis—with the highest standard of living. Life is as controlled as could be. Life back in the early days of the 20th century were far harsher and less forgiving, so it is telling that leaders in the 21st century are viewed to be less trustworthy than those that worked in harder times.

If one goes to the start of the story of J. Williard Marriott, his father had him working on their sugar beet farm from a very early age.

"My father gave me the responsibility of a man," said Marriott many years later. "He would tell me what he wanted done, but never said much about how to do it. It was up to me to find out for myself" (108).

By the age of 13, Marriott was already starting to be entrepreneurial by growing and selling lettuce from a few fallow acres on their farm. By the time he finished university, he already had plans for his own business. He secured the A&W franchise for Washington, DC, including Baltimore and Richmond, and headed east in the spring of 1927. Marriott and partner Hugh Colton pooled 6,000 U.S. dollars to buy equipment and rent space for their tiny operation. On May 20, 1927, the duo opened their nine-stool root beer stand at 3128 14th Street, NW.

Today, if a graduate from university wanted to start a business, they would probably be told it was too early, and that they should first gain experience. The underlying point was that there was an understanding and acceptance of taking risk in order to get ahead that was stronger in the 1920s than arguably today. In fairness, this is a relatively recent change as the 1980s was a period renowned for many young entrepreneurs taking chances. The shift to discourage risk arguably grew with greater focus on modern business values, which in turn have generated a more conservative approach.

For 58 years, J. Willard Marriott went on to build the Marriott business. He was known to work every hour and be passionate about his business.

Just before his death in 1985, J. Willard Marriott summed up the personal philosophy that drove him his entire life: "A man should keep on being constructive and do constructive things. He should take part in the things that go on in this wonderful world. He should be someone to be reckoned with. He should live life and make every day count, to the very end. Sometimes it's tough. But that's what I'm going to do" (109).

Conrad Hilton

Hilton became known as "the inn keeper to the world" (110). This is a title that does demonstrate how large an influence Hilton has had on the hospitality industry. However, he was much more than just a businessman, but similar to Marriott, he was dedicated to charitable causes and the importance of his people. His leadership style, values, and approach, especially the company culture, give a clear picture about the person who led the Hilton Hotels' for over 30 years. He faced many adversities while trying to start his hotel empire, especially because he was so new to the industry and lacked experience. The struggles of the great depression led to him losing almost everything and needing to start all over again. By 1946, Hilton was back on his feet and slowly repurchased the hotels he lost during the depression and started the Hilton Corporation.

He used his charisma to motivate employees so that staff could provide a quality service to guests. He had been known to lead a group of people under his inspiration, passion, and vision. He was detail-oriented and had a strong business sense. He worked with employees to implement a more transformational leadership style that showed he cared for the employees. In order to guide individuals to perform better on their job, Hilton paid attention to his employees' concerns and mentored them. During Hilton's leading period, he enhanced the communication between subordinates and him so that employees could better express their opinions. Even though controversies existed, Hilton would tolerate differences when he thought employees' views were constructive.

It is worth noting that both Marriott and Hilton were accessible and visible as leaders—something that today, many say, is missing. It is said that today, business is more sophisticated than ever before. It is certainly more controlled by the level of distrust in leaders, which is at a record high, and it is not hard to argue that we see far fewer such characters able to build empires as these figures once did.

Is leadership today better? The stats say not. Is business better managed?

It could be argued that hospitality business leaders, because of the very business that they are in, have a head start over many political and other business leaders. To be drawn into the hospitality industry, one would fairly expect that there is already a passion for service and people. The industry relies on the importance of its people, its teams, and how they perform. The fact that leadership has been called into question is a major concern in its own right and the importance of this text.

Hospitality is about being hospitable and caring for the well-being of the guests. It is about creating experiences that do make guests feel safe and create either an escape from daily life or an environment that a guest wants to experience again. Talk to anyone in any walk of life and they will recall, with a smile, a great culinary experience, a memorable night in a hotel, a special moment of shared love in a restaurant or hotel, or even a great evening with friends spent together. Hospitality is the framework that does create lasting memories.

It is testament to both Marriott and Hilton that their legacies have been long lasting and global. For decades, many have been proud to be employees of these organizations, and both companies have had the strongest of cultures developed over many decades. Hilton and Marriott are arguably the fathers of the global hotel companies that really did internationalize the industry.

An Industry Founded on a Desire to Serve and Create Experiences

There have been many articles written in recent times that argue that customers today are looking for hotels that offer genuine experiences that are memorable. There has been a move toward creating urban resorts such as the Ned Hotel in the City of London, which boasts 13 restaurants and a private members club to new retreats and resorts where the guest has no need to leave the premises.

This is viewed as fresh thinking, but in truth, this has long been at the heart of the industry, which was, in essence, founded to create great experiences.

London's First Hotel

"I don't want to go to heaven, I want to go to Claridge's" (Spencer Tracey) (111).

The first hotels really emerged after the French Revolution, when many of the great servants, chefs, butlers, and housekeepers within the aristocratic households fled abroad. It was natural that they would flee to new locations and create a new landscape for hospitality establishments. Many of the great chefs and butlers fled all across Europe. It can be fairly argued that the French Revolution was the catalyst for the growth of the modern hotel industry we know today, although clearly, there was still a long period of evolution to take place.

In the United Kingdom, the first real modern hotel was opened in Exeter (in the South West of England in the late 1790s), but London's first genuine hotel of note was to open in 1812. It was later to become known as Claridge's (112), but when it first opened, it operated under the name *Mivart's Hotel* (113) and was run by James Mivart. It originally provided by-the-month accommodation for the wealthy visitors who came to London for lengthy periods.

William and Marianna Claridge had served in noble households; William as a butler. They managed to accumulate enough to buy a small hotel on Brook Street, which they steadily grew. They then purchased Mivart's Hotel in 1854.

The hotel, under both Mivart and later the Claridge's, brought a new level of service and hospitality to the capital city. Until this point, it had been the great gentleman's clubs that had dominated the scene, but these two began to change the landscape, and the growth of great hotels began in London. They brought new levels of service to the fore that attracted the most senior and elite of clienteles.

Mivarts had already built a strong reputation. Prior to his ascension to the throne, the flamboyant King George IV was said to have had a suite permanently reserved, while the monarchs of Russia and the Netherlands were among many distinguished guests who came to enjoy the hotel's legendary luxury. With the change of ownership and name, the hotel's reputation continued to soar unabated. In 1860, Empress Eugenie of France stayed at Claridge's and was visited by none other than Queen Victoria and Prince Albert. This in itself was the best advertising the hotel could have received, and soon, the hotel was the place to be seen and to stay.

Mivart and Claridge were the trailblazers and, of course, Claridge's is still one of the great hotels today. However, the London hotel scene was really transformed by Richard D'Oyly Carte who brought both new thinking and hospitality expertise to London when he built The Savoy Hotel next to his own theater. It seems so logical to build a hotel next to one's own theater, but it was a visionary move at the time.

Richard D'Oyly Carte: Innovator and Showman

Richard D'Oyly Carte was already famed as the driving force behind the comic operas of Gilbert and Sullivan, which were being performed across the world.

Richard D'Oyly Carte began his career as a theatrical agent in 1870. His association with W. S. Gilbert and Arthur Sullivan began in 1875 when he was appointed manager of the Royalty Theater in Dean Street, Soho. To supplement the main entertainment of Jacques Offenbach's La Périchole, he encouraged the composer Sullivan to write a score for Gilbert's comic libretto, *Trial by Jury*. First performed on March 25, 1875, it proved an immediate success, enjoying a run of 131 performances.

Correctly forecasting that there would be more hits to come, Carte formed *Mr D'Oyly Carte's Opera Company*, which went on to present every subsequent work by Gilbert and Sullivan, from *The Sorcerer* (1877), through *HMS Pinafore* (1878), *Pirates of Penzance* (1879), *Patience* (1881), *Iolanthe* (1882), to *The Mikado* (1885) and *The Gondoliers* (1889).

Carte's long-held ambition of establishing a "permanent abode for light opera" in London came to fruition on October 10, 1881, when he opened the Savoy Theater on the Strand, with a performance of *Patience*. Built to designs by C. J. Phipps, it was claimed it was the first public building in the world to be lit entirely by electricity. The luxurious Savoy Hotel—a new business venture by Carte, built on a vacant plot of land next to the Savoy Theater, and designed by Thomas Edward Colcutt—opened its doors in 1889, and with César Ritz as manager and Auguste Escoffier (114) as head chef, went on to become the favorite meeting place of London's high society, led by the Prince of Wales. The hotel boasted a number of innovations such as electric lights and lifts, and its bar was the first in London to serve cocktails. It proved an enormous financial success and enabled Carte to buy other hotels, including Claridge's.

The Savoy was founded by three of the greatest talents of the time; Richard D'Oyly Carte, along with the great hotelier Cesar Ritz and the leading chef, Auguste Escoffier. Together, they did set and create new benchmarks. Ritz may be best known as the name that sits above the Ritz Hotel, but his greatness was founded in his years at The Savoy. Escoffier, in turn, was known as "the king of chefs and the chef of kings" (115). Together, they created a new standard and excitement that helped build the momentum for the Grand Hotels to follow.

Rosa Lewis: The First Lady of Hotels

There have always been great female figures in business, and Rosa Lewis (116) was one of the dominant figures of her day. Rosa came to the fore as she was exceptionally skilled in cooking and entertaining. She became a confidant to many of London's leading social figures and earned their trust and admiration.

She was born in 1867, left school at the age of 12, and entered domestic service and first came to note as running the kitchens of the Duc d'Orleans at Sandhurst. With her skills for producing a lighter French style of cooking, she soon became hugely popular with the society hostesses of the time and was invited to cook in fashionable private houses for dinner parties.

It was through her cooking that Rosa was linked to Edward VII. Edward loved great food, and great parties, so it was natural that two would form a bond. He was the making of her, and her services became the height of fashion. This connection, and Rosa's life, formed the outline of the popular 1970s BBC TV series *The Duchess of Duke Street* (117).

After marrying butler Chiney Lewis in 1893, the couple moved to Eaton Terrace, and in 1902, purchased the already fashionable Cavendish

Hotel. Here, Rosa welcomed American millionaires and distinguished English families such as the Churchills, Asquiths, and Saviles, many of whom she had worked for previously. With the outbreak of the First World War, society entertaining came to an end, and Rosa turned her attentions to welcoming impoverished military officers to the Cavendish. Her kind and tolerant nature never allowed them to pay, and with her tactics of allowing rich guests to cover the costs of the poor, she managed to continue these charitable efforts until her death.

Lord Forte

Lord Forte's importance was immeasurable in many ways. He was very similar to both Marriott and Hilton, in that he understood the value of people and teams, but what makes him stand apart is that he was, in truth, an Italian immigrant who became a grandee of British society, becoming a close friend of the Prime Minister, Margaret Thatcher.

He was born in the village of Monforte in Italy and arrived in the United Kingdom with his mother at the age of four, learning his first English in Alloa, Clackmannanshire, where his father ran a cafe—called the Savoy. His education was partly at Alloa academy and Dumfries college as a boarder, and then for two years in Rome, after which the young Forte re-joined his family, who had moved to Weston-super-Mare, where his father was running a cafe with two cousins.

However, he always had the urge to set up his own business, despite the unfriendly economic environment of the 1930s. His first venture was to create a milk bar on London's Regent Street. It was not initially successful, but he reduced his staff levels and expanded into the shop next door. It was brave move that few would have taken. By 1938, Forte owned five milk bars in London.

During the Second World War, Forte was interned on the Isle of Man because of his Italian nationality, but Forte was released three months later to become an adviser to the Ministry of Food.

The real catalyst for the growth of Forte's empire came in the unlikely form of the 1951 Festival of Britain, which earned him some great profits from catering for the festival that were then reinvested into property.

The 1950s saw a great property boom from which many astute business-men did prosper, Forte included.

Fueled by the profits from catering for the festival, he began buying London hotels, beginning with the Waldorf in 1958, and by 1970, Sir Charles Forte (as he became that year) controlled Britain's biggest hotel chain.

Forte's leap to the top of the hotel ladder came through a takeover of Trust Houses in 1970. The company interests included the Café Royal, Forte's personal favorite acquisition, almost 250 hotels in Britain and Ireland, the Henekey Inns, Quality Inns, Kardomah coffee houses, the Travelodge chain of motels in America, Canada, Mexico, and Tahiti, and motorway service stations. It was also in charge of catering at 24 European airports, as well as the Lord Mayor's banquet in London, the Edinburgh festival, and the UN in New York.

Paul Bocuse: The Lion of Lyon

Paul Bocuse was nicknamed *The Chef of the Century*, and there is little argument that he had a major impact on global food styles and cookery in the last 50 years. He was one of the first celebrity chefs, was a key figure in popularizing the nouvelle cuisine movement of lighter and seasonal fare, and created an international cooking contest called the Culinary Olympics.

The Culinary Olympics was founded to bring international competition, outside of France, which was often a closed shop in its competitions, to chefs from all around the world. The latest contest, in February 2020, attracted 67 countries to compete, with Norway coming away with the major award.

Bocuse understood that hospitality was global. His heart always remained in Lyon, but he understood the need to inspire talent all across the world. There are very few chefs who have had as great an impact on a City's standing. Lyon and Paul Bocuse were closely aligned. They were soulmates. Bocuse helped transform Lyon into one of the most decorated culinary destinations in Europe. In the process, he became the most influential French chef of his generation. Few will visit Lyon and be unaware of his influence. His success earned him the nickname the *Lion of Lyon*.

However, he was not limited to Lyon and worked all across the world. He co-founded restaurants at Epcot and Disneyland Paris and was affiliated with nearly 20 others from Europe to Asia. In 1969, he helped plan the menu for the inaugural Concorde flight, perhaps the first meal ever officially dubbed *nouvelle cuisine*. He was the first truly commercial chef in terms of lending his name to a full range of products.

Paul Bocuse was arguably not a man for the *me too* generation, as he was old-fashioned in his views and well known for his love of women.

"Food and sex have much in common," he told The *Daily Telegraph*. "*We* consummate a union, we devour each other's eyes, we hunger for one other." Adding that food and sexual intercourse were the essentials in life, he explained, "I realize my vision is a little macho, but I am a man of my time and believe that whatever they say, women love men to be macho" (118).

As is often the way, his public comments hid a more complex and private character, which was known to care deeply for those under his charge. He understood the need to be controversial and a character for commercial reasons, but his true passion was his restaurants and food.

Bocuse was born into the industry. His family had been innkeepers dating back to 1765. For much of his youth, the Bocuses ran a smaller bistro.

French cuisine had gone through many phases over the centuries, and the general characteristics of nouvelle cuisine being farm-fresh ingredients, shorter cooking times, and delicate sauces had already crept into the cuisine by the time Bocuse gained renown in the 1960s, but Bocuse became its champion and promoter.

His mission, he said, was to "render unto a chicken that which is its due, and nothing more" (119). Another time, he likened his cooking to a "slender young girl in a see-through blouse" (120) compared with the "heavily corseted 1900 beauties" of grand French cuisine.

In 1961, he earned his first Michelin star. A second star followed in 1962, then a third in 1965, indicating that the restaurant, in the guide's parlance, offers *exceptional cuisine* and is *worth a special journey*.

In 1975, French President Valéry Giscard d'Estaing bestowed on Mr. Bocuse the Legion of Honor. It was the first time the award had been given to a chef. The ceremony was memorable for Bocuse wore not a formal suit, but his chef's jacket and sky-high toque.

Paul Bocuse teamed with Disney again in 2014 to open a bistro at the Paris theme park, Bistrot Chez Rémy, inspired by the animated feature film *Ratatouille*, about a rat who is a master chef.

In 1987, Mr. Bocuse created the Bocuse d'Or, a cooking contest held every two years and featuring competing teams from 24 countries. In 1990, he opened a culinary arts school in Ecully, France. He genuinely believed in the importance of inspiring talent for the future and from across the world.

Common Lessons

Of course, these great figures are just a few of the many industry greats, but the point is that all have common factors that link them together. All had a genuine passion for service and love for the industry. All had an understanding of the importance of people in hospitality, both guests and employees. One could talk business models to them, and one suspects that they would all argue that great hospitality businesses are founded on core pillars such as good locations, great service, good people, great food, reasonable price, and creating experiences that customers would want to purchase. These factors have been the same from the days of Rosa Lewis, William Claridge through to the days of Conrad Hilton, and to the modern era of Ken McCulloch, regarded by many as one of the industry's finest entrepreneurs (121). One suspects that all would argue that success comes from great people performing well to deliver great experiences to guests, and arguably, this is what sets them apart to leave real legacies that have and will last the test of time.

However, a deeper point is that all were innovators. William Claridge took service to a new level. Richard D'Oyly was the first to link theater and hotels together to create exceptional experiences. Rosa Lewis became a confidant of kings and aristocracy, but also showed a rare care for the vulnerable. Ken McCulloch founded boutique hotel brands focusing on experience. Hilton was the first hotel group to introduce televisions into each of their rooms. He initially struggled and failed before building his empire. He took his lessons, adapted, and came back. Pierre Bellon's success came from seeing the decline in shipbuilding in Marseille, which gave him the motivation to adapt and find a new career. J. Williard Marriott and his wife started initially with a coffee shop before building an empire of hotels, restaurants, and in food services. Lord Forte's story is not far different. They all built strong businesses through innovation and entrepreneurship to a level few have seen in recent years.

They also all understood the importance of culture and people to a high level. Business may be more sophisticated today, but people are also more disengaged, and there is less loyalty. It is hard to argue that business is better managed today.

There is a desire for change. There is a desire for new leadership to emerge, which does once again place people at the heart of success and perhaps build companies such as the ones stated.

The End of the Second World War—the Inspiration to New Thinking and Globalization

As we write about history, it is also correct that we note the importance of the Second World War on creating a new psychology within business. The Second World War plays a bigger role throughout this book, as it created, following the war itself, an illustration of the kind of leadership that many desire to see a return to. Of course, the world never can turn back time, but there are clear lessons that can be re-examined in a new context. It may even be an apt comparison, as so many have compared the rebuilding process facing the industry post-COVID, as being similar to that faced after the Second World War.

It is something rarely written about, but it was the Second World War that did open up the world as one for global business and laid the ground for the great international hotel groups that grew in the 1950s and 1960s.

It is one of the strange contradictions about war, as it often is the catalyst for new horizons to follow, both economically and socially. After the Great War of 1914–1918, there was an era of prosperity that followed in the 1920s. The 1920s too were viewed to be a period of a lighter social mood, which of course was followed by the more somber economic fall in the 1930s, which arguably lay the ground for the rise of Hitler and his brand of socialism in Germany.

The decade following the Second World War is fondly remembered as a period of economic growth and cultural stability. The war had been won, and this gave many a renewed sense of pride and belief. The hardships of the previous 15 years of war and depression were gradually replaced by rising living standards, increased opportunities, and a newly emerging culture that was more confident of its future and place in the world. Both in the United Kingdom and United States, new ground was broken. The founding of the National Health Service (NHS), new social agendas, and a greater overall social consciousness emerged.

One will often hear politicians referring back to these days as they seek to make a case for their agendas. However, a closer examination of the actual events of the immediate post-war period provides a picture that is much more complex and in contradiction with the world view that government intervention is the essential ingredient of prosperity. There are parallels to today's landscape.

In the United Kingdom, almost at every election, there is a battleground over the NHS. The Labor Party see the NHS as an important part of their legacy from the Atlee Government, which followed the war. The Conservatives always vow to protect it. It has for a long period of time, even more so during the coronavirus lockdown, been the center ground of debate. It represents compassionate society and was the invention of life post-war. And, 75 years on and still it is arguably the most visible example of compassionate service to all.

In the 2009 State of the Union address (122), President Obama likened his stimulus plan to earlier popular government initiatives, using post-Second World War references: "In the wake of war and depression, the GI Bill sent a generation to college and created the largest middle class in history . . . Government didn't supplant private enterprise; it catalysed private enterprise."

Nobel prize winner and liberal *New York Times* columnist Paul Krugman has also extolled the role of government in the Second World War and the post-Second World War recovery, claiming that "World War II was, above all, a burst of deficit-financed government spending . . . [that]

created an economic boom . . . [that] laid the foundation for long-run prosperity" (123).

There is certainly a strong argument, but it does rather over-estimate the role of government and underestimate the new motivation and energy within business to create economic prosperity. It is one of the realities of modern politics that political leaders will lay claim to economic success and sidestep economic failure as being all outside of their control due to global influences.

Economic Growth Post-Second World War

At the time, both the United States and United Kingdom, as were most of Europe, deeply concerned by the level of debt that they all carried. The standard thinking of the day was most countries would return back to, at best, a deep recession, but the big difference was that there was both greater levels of skills within leaders, within management, and greater motivation within communities to rebuild.

Of course, government funding was of real importance, and it was at the center of creating a genuine social consciousness to a level that had not been witnessed previously, but it was only one part of the equation. The psychology of those in work has also changed. Leaders and managers were more worldly, more broadly experienced, and had a desire to build prosperity. Employees too wanted to come together as communities and showed a new level of compassion and care for one another. It was all this together that gave a new impetus to economic growth. It is fairer to argue that it was the result of lessons from war and the need to find better.

In 1944, the U.S. government spending at all levels accounted for 55 percent of gross domestic product (GDP). By 1947, the government spending had dropped 75 percent in real terms, or from 55 percent of GDP to just over 16 percent of GDP. Over roughly the same period, federal tax revenues fell by only around 11 percent. Gross private investment rose by 223 percent in real terms, with a six-fold real increase in residential-housing expenditures. This surpassed all expectations and maybe illustrated best a new sense of belief that existed across the population. Just as important, the double-digit unemployment rates that had bedeviled the pre-war economy did not return.

It was certainly a stronger position that many expected. It was not that all the economic forecasts were wrong; it was simply that they did not take into account a genuine desire to place the bad days behind and to build something new. Business had new skilled managers, managers who had learned how to respond to setbacks and adversity under war conditions, and this mindset lay the ground for business to excel beyond the forecasts.

A poll of business executives in 1944 and 1945 revealed that only 8.5 percent of them thought the prospects for their company had worsened in the post-war period (123).

A contemporary chronicler noted that in 1945–1946 businesses "had a large and growing volume of unfilled orders for peacetime products" (124).

It is true that the release in wartime economic controls coincided with one of the largest periods of economic growth in U.S. history.

It may even be a lesson to remember for the future—that out of the darkest of times comes new skills that will propel both society and business forward. The Second World War, as terrible as it was, was an inspiration that propelled hospitality into a new age.

PART V

Studies in Leadership

Gioele Camarlinghi—International Hotelier

Leadership in hospitality is a privilege. We have such great people within our Industry who have a passion to serve our guests. My role is to be the Captain of the ship that really does play an important, and yet often unseen, role in making guests feel safe, able to relax, to find their place for respite from the pressures of daily life. We create memories. We bring people together. We serve our communities. It is a privilege to do this.

(Gioele Camarlinghi)

Gioele exemplifies the essence of a true hotelier, a man who cares deeply about the teams that he leads and the guests he serves. He is not one of the biggest names in the industry, but he is one of the most true of hoteliers; one who understands the responsibility of being a general manager and takes great pride in the role that he fulfills every day. A hotelier needs to have a love for running teams, which are like a dysfunctional family, to deliver a service of excellence. The leader is father, mother, confessionary, priest, teacher, and firefighter, all in the same day at times. He or she must have an eye for detail, and an eye for the customer who wants to feel special. Being a hotelier is a unique challenge.

It is, therefore, only right that the first profile of a leader is that of a man who meets all these criteria and will never be found complaining as to his lot.

During the early part of 2020, as Italy went into lockdown and the United Kingdom was still weeks from the same situation, Gioele was staying with his wife and children at his home close to Regents Park in London. He knew though he was going to have to leave them to return to oversee hotels in Milan. Some would have stayed in London, but this thought never crossed his mind. "A captain needs to be on the bridge and there is no excuse if he is not," he said, and so, he returned to Milan with no knowledge of when or if he may next see his family and in full knowledge that Lombardy at that time was directly in harm's way. That is the measure of the man.

If you wish to meet a man who loves to run hotels and lead teams, then Gioele Camarlinghi is a man who does exemplify these traits.

When one meets Gioele, he will greet you formally and with the utmost courtesy, but soon, he will be gently laughing and enjoying the conversation. He loves people as much as he loves hotels, and he has a long record of developing talent under his care. He is fiercely loyal to his friends and in wanting to ensure that the hotel and team together excel to delight guests.

Gioele is a dynamic and determined results-orientated individual with more than 25 years' experience in the hospitality industry. Gioele describes himself as a born organizer and a master motivator; he has succeeded in building team spirit among his staff while implementing exacting service standards. He thrives in a fast-paced environment where his ability to achieve goals while using his strong interpersonal skills come into play.

Gioele is Italian born and bred; he grew up and lived in Florence until he completed his education. At just 14 years old, Gioele was waiting tables at a local hostelry, and he said with a smile on his face that "being a waiter was not a respected trade in those days." Once he finished school, he studied sociology at the university, as he had a fascination with studying people.

Following university, Gioele joined a hotel chain, initially in sales and later in food and beverage. From this position, he was soon promoted to general manager with Jolly Hotels (St. Ermins) in London, and he then moved to Brussels for a year. In 2006, he joined Melia in Paris as the Director of Operations managing nine properties. He was subsequently appointed Area Vice President at Boutique by Melia, and in 2010, he took up a role for Melia overseeing the United Kingdom. Today, he is now back in his native Italy, overseeing a number of leading hotels in Milan and working with the Italian Government.

> For me, true hotel management is about developing a team that the guest not only trusts but likes to be with. Service sits at my heart and I love how hotels offer guests an experience that they will never forget. It is something that lives in the memory for years.

However, to achieve such emotion requires the right team. Hospitality is all about people. Any general manager is only as good as any of the individual staff member they lead. The guest's experience relies on great service, so it is all about people and the environment. The more that we empower the team to play their part and enjoy their work, the guest will enjoy their stay. "My job is to inspire our people to be the best they can be and to enjoy their work. I am a coach, a conductor, a parent, a confident and a chef all rolled into one."

Innovation and creative thinking sit at the heart of this hotelier's vision. Gioele has a traditional hotel in architecture and furnishings and has cleverly and seamlessly mixed this with the avant-garde and the contemporary.

> I do love hotels. They often have a great history and legacy, which gives us a strong story to tell. We bring together this heritage and combine it with modern and creative art styles—we have set the stage in a way that is distinctly different to other hotels and which will challenge the senses of the guest.

As a case study, it is good to open with Gioele, for he is almost a classical hotelier in many ways who really does view the running of a great hotel as an honor and privilege. It does make the man stand apart from others.

Gioele Camarlinghi

Abigail Tan, CEO—The St. Giles Hotel Group
Believing in the Human Touch that Hotels Can Play—for the Guest,
for Employees and for Communities

It is true that the stories of most leading players all across the industry will normally follow a certain route and be relatively predictable. It is all very natural as careers do evolve along a designated path. However, one cannot say the same in relation to Abigail Tan, the CEO of the St. Giles Group of Hotels, but not for the reason that many may initially think. It is true that her family has a long history within the hospitality industry, one which Abigail has followed, but she is very much anything but either predictable or stereotypical.

We live in a world where it is well known that many feel disengaged, where many are struggling to find purpose and feel lost and struggling with mental health issues. There has been a growing voice for a more compassionate approach to leadership one that does return to the old-fashioned principles where businesses did play a central role in the lives of employees and communities. Many argue that this has been impossible with the ever-increasing demands of many owners and asset managers. Abigail Tan may well see another road forward.

She is arguably one of the modern leaders to emerge who does possess a real belief that hotels play a central role in communities and where the human connection that hotels create is a central part of the brand. She is the modern CEO in many ways, but has an almost old-fashioned belief in the importance of employees and guests as being almost part of an extended family. It is very rare to see this in an age that has been dominated by brands and where many employees have felt disengaged from their employers.

Most articles one will read about Abigail will portray her extrovert side; how she flies a helicopter, plays the electric guitar, is skilled in boxing, has run marathons, abseils down buildings for charity, and rides a motorcycle. Reading her press, she does sound as almost a modern version of Mrs. Peel from *The Avengers*. However, this is just one part of the story. The following aims to tell the story of a modern leader with a genuine passion and heart for the industry and her people.

Abigail grew up Malaysia and gained exposure to the hotel industry from a young age. In fact, her family has been running hotels for three generations. Her grandfather and uncle ran one of Malaysia's real estate dynasties, and her father is now the managing director of the publicly listed IGB Corporation, the parent company of St. Giles Hotels Group, which owns nine hotels and has plans for growing the group to 20 hotels all across the world.

Abigail joined the St. Giles Hotels team as the director of corporate affairs and strategic investments in 2009, involved with the purchase of two New York properties and assisting with negotiations and transition preparations. In 2014, she became St. Giles Hotels' Head of United Kingdom, Europe, and North America, and in 2018, was promoted to the chief executive officer.

Abigail holds an undergraduate degree in business management and a master's degree with distinction in international management and innovation from the University of Exeter.

How is the story of Abigail different?

Much has been written about the desire of many to see a new style in leadership come to the fore, one that has an eye on the role of hotels within communities, one that once again does place people at the heart of the business, and one that is progressive in thinking. It is in these areas that Abigail has already been working.

It can be argued that Abigail does represent the future, progressive style of leadership that many are seeking. She would be modest and disagree, but then again, that is partly Abigail's approach. She does not seek public relations (PR) and recognition, although she understands that it is part of her role. She is more focused on building a business and brand that has substance and where her teams feel proud to work.

Although stories focus on Abigail's all-action approach, she is, in truth, equally focused on the detail mechanics of running a hotel. She is as happy working with the back of house teams and teams on the floor as being the public leader. She knows the detail of her operations, and one should not be fooled by her quiet, kindly manner as she is, as one would expect from her sporting endeavors, both steely determined combined with having a strong knowledge base.

More importantly, she has built a belief and pride in her teams that the hotels and business do stand for something more and bigger, that they do possess real purpose.

At the heart of Abigail's story is a genuine love that she has for hotels. She also understands the very human connection that does play between employee and guest as well as between communities at large and the company and her teams. She has an innate belief that hotels should never lose sight of what makes them special—the human touch. She views a hotel as almost a home for guests and an important place where they are treated with care, and her employees treated as part of an extended family.

A good example is their foundation called *Hotels with Heart*. It is not seen as a separate corporate social responsibility (CSR) program, but it is a core part of the culture of the brand. They have pulled together a team that is comprised of volunteers, activists, fundraisers, sponsors, and mentors. They are the advocates of change. More importantly, there is a genuine sense of pride that the teams have in playing a key role within local communities and with local charities.

It will be interesting to observe how Abigail takes the company forward, but one suspects very successfully, as she seems so in tune with the desires and expectations of both the guest and employees. If she can continue to do this, then she will have a very influential business that can be a role model for many others across the world.

Abigial Tan

Sir Richard Branson
The dyslexic who became a global icon

British entrepreneur Sir Richard Branson is a face that is almost instantly recognizable. He is the face of the Virgin brand, and interestingly, is one of the most trusted business figures around. Branson's business empire has been involved in managing train franchises, airlines, record companies, hotels across the world, sports and leisure companies, pensions, broadband, and even space travel, to name just a few. He is able to leap barriers and be accepted in a way that very few could ever achieve.

Richard Branson was born in 1950 in Surrey, England. His father, Edward James Branson, was a barrister. His mother, Eve Branson, was employed as a flight attendant. Richard, who struggled with dyslexia, found his time in school very difficult. He went to a leading boarding school, including Stowe, but dropped out at the age of 16 to start a youth-culture magazine called *Student*. The publication, run by students, sold 8,000 U.S. dollars' worth of advertising in its first edition, launched in 1966. The first run of 50,000 copies was disseminated for free, with Branson covering the costs through advertising. Branson's story had begun.

The above example alone is central as it is very unlikely that such a young talent could have the same opportunity to be successful today. For whatever reason, the young Branson clearly felt enabled in a way which is not seen today. Some may counter with the example of Greta Thunberg but she is the face of a cause, not an entrepreneurial, competitive business.

By 1969, Branson was living in a London commune, surrounded by the British music scene. It was during this time that Branson had the idea to begin a mail-order record company called Virgin to help fund his magazine efforts. The company performed modestly, but well enough for Branson to expand his business venture, with a record shop on Oxford Street, London. With the success of the new store, he was able to build a recording studio in 1972 in Oxfordshire, England. The first artist on the Virgin Records label, Mike Oldfield, recorded his single *Tubular Bells* in 1973. The record was an instant smash, staying on the UK charts for 247 weeks. Oldfield became a household name and there was no holding Branson back from this moment.

Using the momentum of Oldfield's success, Branson then signed other aspiring musical groups to the label, including the Sex Pistols. Artists such as the Culture Club, the Rolling Stones, and Genesis would follow, helping to make Virgin Music one of the top six record companies in the world.

Branson did show a real understanding of people's tastes, fashion, and talent. The Sex Pistols was a brave, but Branson showed a unique level of skill and bravado to be able to attract The Rolling Stones and Genesis to virgin.

Branson expanded his entrepreneurial efforts yet again, this time to include the Voyager Group travel company in 1980, the Virgin Atlantic airline in 1984, and a series of Virgin Megastores. However, Branson's success was not always predictable, and by 1992, Virgin was suddenly struggling to stay financially afloat. The company was sold later that year to Thorn EMI for one billion U.S. dollars.

In 1993, he founded the station Virgin Radio, and in 1996, he started a second record company, V2, which signed artists such as Powder Finger and Tom Jones.

Branson has become the acceptable and arguably inspirational face on entrepreneurship for a generation. He has been a figurehead and role model for thousands, showing that you are able to compete with the corporate players and achieve great things. His ongoing battle with British Airways has almost become legendary, and there is little doubt that he changed perceptions and broke new ground in many areas. Branson for many years, decades even, could do little wrong.

Interestingly, the coronavirus is perhaps the first time that he has really been under fire with the PR running against him as he has sought government support for Virgin Airways. Many have argued that he should first place his own assets on the line without fully understanding the levels of funding involved. He has worked, almost without question for 30 years, and that alone is a testament to the man. Maybe the tide is turning; only time will tell. If it has, he has been a pioneer that all should still admire, for he achieved things that few else, if anyone, could do.

Branson wrote the following in 2017, and the words probably do sit at the heart of his philosophy (110):

The road to success is paved with tests,

So you've got to believe in yourself above the rest.
Dream big, and let your passion shine,
If you don't, you won't end up with a dime.
Challenge the status quo, disrupt the market and say YES!
And remember that innovation is an endless quest.
Don't forget to change business for good,
If you want to change the world then you should.
If you think with your head and listen to your heart,
I promise you'll get off to a flying start.
Make bold moves, but always play fair,
Always say please and thank you—it's cool to care.
Do what you love and love what you do,
This advice is nothing new.
Now, stop worrying about whether your business will be a hit,
Rise to the challenge and say "screw it, let's do it!" (125)
Richard Branson

Ken McCulloch—Mr. Glasgow, the founder of the Boutique Hotel Brand

Ken McCulloch's story is very much closely entwined with that of Glasgow. They almost both rose to prominence together. Glasgow has, of course, a long and rich history but back in the 1960s and 1970s, it was viewed as a rugged, often brutal city. At the time, the city's story was dominated by its two leading football teams, Celtic and Rangers. The two teams were not just rivals, but also were split on religious grounds, one representing the catholic community and the other the protestant community. It may seem strange today, but in the 1960s, this created genuine tension and division.

In 1967, Celtic became the first British team to win the European Cup in Lisbon, which really did raise the profile of the city. However, it also heightened tensions between two clubs.

Ken grew up in this era. He has a strong and great love for the city, and it is almost that Glasgow and Ken both became world-class operations in unison.

Ken McCulloch (55) has been described as the one true entrepreneur in the modern hotel industry. There will be those who dispute this claim, but there is no doubt that he certainly does view hotels very differently to most. He wants his hotels to be a home for his guests and works hard to create spaces that will appeal. He arguably has used design within hotels far more effectively than most. However, his greatest skill is that he can see the customer experience through the eyes of the customer, which is a very rare quality indeed. He also views a hotel as almost a theater show and understands that the customer needs to feel engaged, from the moment they walk to the doorstep to the moment they leave. He wants to make his guests feel as though they have truly felt cared for to a level that is hard to find.

Another of Ken's great skills is to entrust young talent, and they, in turn, will go the extra mile for the great man.

Ken will always be working on four or five new boutique hotel brand concepts in his mind—all ready for future development. He will travel, always looking for the small things that will make his hotels better and which will add to the experience and inspire his guests.

Ken will be most famed for being the founder of the boutique hotel brand that really did take off during the 1980s. One Devonshire Gardens broke the mold in many ways. The late 1980s saw the rise of a number of great boutique hotels in the United Kingdom such as Blakes and the Capital Hotel in London, and of course, One Devonshire Gardens. It set a new tone in Glasgow, and the story surrounding Ken moved to another level.

Ken is, in hospitality terms, Mr. Glasgow as he has, over the years, created a series of great venues in the city, bars, restaurants, and hotels, which all broke barriers in their time—One Devonshire Gardens, Malmaison, The Granary, La Bonne Auberge, Charlie Parker's.

Scotland may be best known for some of its great hotels such as Gleneagles, The Old Course Hotel at St. Andrews, Balmoral, and Turnberry, but Ken has been Scotland's most unique driving force, as he constantly sought to invent new concepts to inspire guests, but also to make Scotland a world-class destination. He is as passionate a Scot as one will find.

It was McCulloch who in 1986 put Glasgow's name on the map as a global destination when he opened the city's first boutique hotel, One Devonshire Gardens, with his award-winning interior designer wife Amanda Rosa and Andrew Fairlie as head chef. Fairlie gained Glasgow's first Michelin star at the hotel in 1996.

McCulloch though will be best known for *Malmaison Hotels*, which set a new benchmark in hotels, making mid market hotels feel comfortable in being stylistically sexy. He launched the group in 1994 and sold it in 1998, going on to launch the five-star Columbus hotel in Monaco.

He then returned to Scotland to create Dakota hotels, which has been another success.

McCulloch has also inspired a generation of high-achieving hoteliers. He has always believed in giving talent an opportunity and many of his protégées have gone onto hold successful senior industry roles.

Ken McCulloch, like Marriott, Hilton, and Forte, before him has a passion for the industry and for hotels that will burn bright till for a long after period of time. He will never retire as he thinks about hotels and of new ideas for how to improve the guest experience 24/7. His parents were involved in the theater, and it had a lasting impact on Ken. He long had the desire to create very special experiences, ones that inspire joy and memories. He understands that running a hotel is a bit like a theater show—the guests wants to be inspired, entertained, and able to leave daily life behind. He used to chuckle that one of his hotels was designed in such a way that it would make "ladies feel naughty," as it made them feel safe and comfortable. He hates the limelight and prefers to be in the background, but his attention to detail is always focused on the guest. One will find Ken personally working on the music playlist for the restaurant and bars in his hotels, thinking about new designs and constantly talking to his teams.

Ken is a very special man who does truly understand the guest and how to create an experience that makes them feel special and valued. He has a way to always make you feel at home, genuinely happy to see you, and interested in what you have to say. He has, in his way, broken many barriers and changed the thinking of the industry during the 1990s and early 2000s. He would not care about this; he cares little for industry recognition, he only cares if his guests and employees feel valued. He thinks on a different plane to many, and he sees small touches in the customer journey that no one else will. He is a man apart.

Ken McCulloch

Marc Verstringhe, Founder of Catering and Allied
A Man for All Seasons—Leading Through Heart and Generosity, Rather than Management Science to Build a Special Business in Its Time.

It is only right to note that the man himself would disagree—and may be rightly so—with what is written. Marc would argue that his business was built on a science and even wrote a book on the subject *Managing to Serve: Learning from Catering & Allied* (Sally Heavens 2002).

However, what made Marc Verstringhe, the founder of Catering and Allied, stand apart was that he had a genuine love and passion for people, food, and hospitality. It was such a genuine passion that anyone who spent time in Marc's company could not fail to be touched by its authenticity. He did not care about gender; he was one of the first to appoint female board directors. Marc was a naturally progressive thinker, as he only saw the service to be provided and how clients responded to women was often far better than to men. He admired the way that many women approached business, and he backed this up by ensuring that were in positions of authority. This was ahead of its time, and he created almost a myth that surrounded the business, which made it competitive. It was even rumored that one company banned the mention of *Catering and Allied* by its employees—a high complement and one that served to underline the aura that the company carried at its height.

Marc was progressive, as he could see a bigger picture, and he was not concerned about gender, politics, or pettiness. If you were good enough, that is all that mattered.

Catering and Allied was a value-based brand before the food service sector became so preoccupied with brands as a concept.

Here lies the heart of story of Marc; he was a man slightly ahead of his time, as his instincts and core behaviors created a business entity that many would admire. Marc talked of the importance of strategic alliances and working together when others focused on themselves. Marc talked of the value of having great people over management structures, while others focused heavily on infrastructures.

For a period, Catering and Allied was viewed as the company that most in London would like to have worked for. It paid higher salaries for its managers and attracted the best talent.

Marc will rightly argue that there was a strategy, plan, and science that stood behind the whole approach to the business, but to the outside eye, it relied on a group of great people who enjoyed working together, who were empowered to be individualistic, and who had a love of food service.

There are probably many articles that have been written that will note that the strongest cultures come from a leadership ethos that is genuine and authentic, one that has a passion for its mission. This was Catering and Allied in its prime. The company's teams had a love for Marc, who they all knew was a generous hearted man, who like all great men had his flaws, but which were easily forgiven by his teams.

This is a story of a company that was sold in the 1990s. Why is it important today?

Because the values and approach that Marc believed in with such strength are exactly what people are looking for today.

Leadership values are often timeless. In times of crisis, people do want something to believe in; something that is bigger than just the company's own interests. Strategic alliances will be of prime importance again as we rebuild, just as will generosity and compassion. Placing people first again over structures may just be the right way forward.

These are the values that many will be looking for as we re-emerge post-crisis. They are not new values, but they are ones that made Marc stand apart from many. It is no coincidence that one will often see Marc still invited to events all across the circuit, for he was an inspiration to many and is still greatly loved by all.

Marc's legacy will live on. The challenge is to make sure that we create similar legacies today that impact similarly on future generations.

For those that scoff and say this was another time, the answer is often lessons repeat themselves, and learning from the past is a valuable asset that is open for all. It is a fair bet that Marc's approach would work just as effectively post-crisis, as it is what many want to follow.

Marc Verstringhe

Raissa and Joyce De Haas, Founders Double Dutch Drinks
Building a Brand Through Being Genuine and Authentic

It is well known that leadership comes in a number of different forms. At the time of writing, the great Heineken company has just taken an equity stake in Double Dutch, which will give the young company and its two leaders real heavyweight strength.

Many view Double Dutch as almost a classic example of an entrepreneurial success story. Charismatic twin sisters who have set up their own business in a very difficult market and today sell their products in over 20 countries across the world have won numerous awards and recognitions, which place many more established companies in the shade. These include:

- Britain's most innovative and disruptive F&B product by Sir Richard Branson in the Foodpreneur Award, 2015
- Retail and E-commerce Forbes 30 Under 30, 2018
- 30 under 30 Best Natural Products, 2018
- SME Business Leader of the year, The Telegraph, 2018
- Winner of Best Premium or Adult Drink at the World Beverage Innovation Awards 2016
- Casual Dining Gold Awards for Innovation in 2017 and 2018
- One to Watch representing the United Kingdom in European Business Awards, 2019
- Food and Drink Entrepreneur of the year, Great British Entrepreneur Awards, 2019
- Voted number one tonic for your G&T by GQ magazine, 2019
- Official mixer partner of the IWSC Awards, 2019
- Awarded silver medals in the Alberta Beverage Awards, 2019
- LDC top 50 Most Ambitious Business Leader
- Voted number 1 in the top 10 women to watch in the drinks industry by #Shestartedit100

It is an impressive list of accolades, but it only tells a small part of the story about Joyce and Raissa de Haas.

One would imagine from the aforementioned that the twin sisters have an excellent strategic approach and a strong team that surrounds them. This may or may not be true, but the heart of their success comes from the fact they do lead from the front, work longer hours than many, are the face of the brand, easily accessible to clients, and are the most unaffected people through their own success. They are the same characters today as they were when they first started the business.

One of the reasons that Double Dutch is so popular is because people just naturally warm to the two leads. They are socially very competent and have a positive outlook toward life. You will rarely hear them ever say a bad word about anyone. I have met them on days when their worlds are fallen apart and on days when they have won one of the mentioned awards, and you would not know the difference. They do, as the old maxim says, accept success and failure in an even temperament. A smile and laugh is never far from the surface, even when they have been in pain.

On saying all this, they are two extremely bright and intelligent modern entrepreneurs. Both with MBAs, but their strong attribute is that they will genuinely lead from the front. Moreover, they are genuine and authentic in the truest sense.

Why is this important?

Very simply, as it builds trust and goodwill with both clients and employees, which, in these times, can be invaluable.

When one talks about leadership, the one message that comes through time and again is that little is more important than trust. It enhances influence and performance. It also builds respect both internally and externally.

It is the X factor of many great entrepreneurial businesses that cannot be copied or followed for the simple reason that one cannot copy another's behaviors with ease. There are many great businesses that have been built on the positive personalities of their lead players. Of course, the product needs to be excellent too, but there are many businesses that have failed even with a great product.

Genuine and authentic people in leadership will add value to a business, in terms of goodwill, that can be immeasurable. It does create an X factor—that accountants may loathe—but will attract the best talent, new customers, and build a momentum in the market.

Double Dutch launched against some very established products and has built a niche in a relatively short period of time. They are already viewed to be success stories, although you will not hear those words come from Joyce and Raissa. In their minds, there is still along path to follow, which is true. However, they now have a platform from which they can build something of real value, and that platform was built through their own characters.

It is a story that is very much worth following.

Raissa and Joyce De Has

Kevin Watson, Managing Director, Amadeus—Part of the NEC Group
It Starts with Character—Never Taking a Backward Step from Trouble, but Nurturing People with Care

At the end of the day, the success of all business leadership is determined by the results and progress of a business. Seasoned leaders will tell you that one of the hardest challenges is to take over the captaincy of a ship that is *troubled* and take it into safe waters, ones where other start to cast envious eyes. This is the role that Kevin Watson has achieved with Amadeus.

Kevin took over as the managing director just as Amadeus was about to embark on catering at the 2012 London Olympics, an event that did show up its shortcomings, with the company making highly publicized losses in the region of eight million pounds. There was little doubt that Kevin faced a major challenge in inheriting the mantle of leadership, and for a while after, Amadeus was not considered as a premium player, but more as the caterer for The NEC Group alone.

Kevin soon started in rebuilding the team, bringing together a team that he could trust and who would be loyal to him. Interestingly he recruited a new senior team of proven players that others may have viewed to have peaked and were past their prime but who Kevin saw both experience and a hunger to prove the doubters wrong. He combined this experience with some younger developing team members and managed both with a strong arm. Within two years, perceptions began to change as the company grew, and within four years, Amadeus was being viewed as *coming players*. Within six years, Amadeus had tripled in size, was returning very good returns, and was now viewed, respectfully, as a premium player. It has been a great achievement, but the facts tell only a small part of the story.

The real story of the turnaround sits with Kevin Watson. Many would simplistically describe Kevin as a high competent managing director, a strong, competitive character who is very driven to succeed. This is all true, but the industry is full of such characters, so what is it that makes Kevin stand apart?

A number of features that many will not easily see without knowing the man himself. From a young age, Kevin has been a natural leader.

He was happy to be accountable and take on responsibility, but more importantly, he is happy to accept the slings and arrows of life without complaint. He will privately tell stories of how the Mafia chained him to a radiator in Rome when he was working for Compass Group or of difficult times managing the major Burger King store in Leicester Square. One will never hear him complaining about these episodes, but instead chuckling about the adventure. This may make Kevin sound like he is full of bravado, which is actually far from the truth—he just accepts that good and bad happen together and would accept both in equal measure. However, the reason he faced such *adventures* was the simple fact that he would not be intimidated nor take a backward step. Perhaps, it is such courage one does need when one has to face tough challenges in a turnaround situation, as, of course, it will not be for the faint of heart. Kevin's ability was to accept the pressures of the moment in a calm objectivity, which has allowed him to handle effectively the difficult moments.

The contradiction is although Kevin is a strong character, he does also have a deep understanding of people, of their failings, and how to bring the best out of a team. This takes a character who does have a strong empathy for others, and that life is full of both good and bad. There are a number of examples where he has taken a person who many believe is on the downward spiral and given them the chance to rekindle their career. He has seen a spark in them that others have not, and as a result, he has found deep loyalty in return.

Loyalty and trust do not just come to a leader because of their position. It comes from a trust that is earned. Kevin thinks deeply about best ways to manage people and works hard to give his team real support, as he knows that they will support him in return.

Finally, he understands the mechanics of a business and enjoys the cut and thrust pressures of building a successful organization. In some ways, he views the building of a business almost as a personal contest, and to be successful, he understands that he cannot do this alone, but needs to build a multilevel approach through his people, his product, and market perception.

When Amadeus faced the low moments of 2012 and 2013 as the fallout from the Olympics hit the public domain, the hard truth of the situation was that Amadeus was not good enough. Kevin would never accept this point publicly, but privately, he would have thought very deeply about how both team and product would need to improve.

Today, one can fairly argue that Amadeus is one of the most innovative companies on the marketplace, showing great leadership in vegan and health food innovation and also a leading role model in tech used in high-volume audiences. This work began almost straight after the Olympics, and it has been building gradually ever since, one step at a time. He has built the multilayered approach, which offers an excellent product that can today compete with any competitor, but also with a team that has great faith in its leadership.

At the end of the day, Kevin's success has come from how he can see a picture. He is one of the deepest thinkers, but he also understands what it does take to build a successful business—both in terms of people and product. He also understands it takes time and a lot of nurturing from the leader. Success never comes quickly, but it does come if one builds the right pillars for it to grow.

Kevin Watson

Ramesh Vala OBE, Global Ambassador, Ince
A Person Who Engages Life Fully Will Also Be the Person Who Enjoys Life Most

Far from being an expert in hospitality, Ramesh is a leading lawyer who is a case study in genuine leadership, acting as one believes is right, not just because one is told to do so. It is important in life to possess a strong set of values and convictions, and there is little doubt that Ramesh is driven by a high set of values, where he understands not only that there is more to life than we all see, but that little is of more importance than trust and relationships.

Ramesh is very much a man who has created his own story. His childhood was spent in Kenya, and he grew up in Nairobi, where amidst hardships, he dreamed of becoming a successful lawyer. Having procured outstanding results in his *A* levels and being recognized as the top all-round student, he found himself at the London School of Economics, thanks to the patronage of a family in Kenya—a concrete step toward realizing his dream. In what was then perhaps an unprecedented feat of achievement in the United Kingdom, Ramesh was made a salaried partner at a sizeable Central London law firm, a mere 18 months after his qualification as a lawyer, and in the next two years, he was an equity partner in a top 100 British law firm—one of only 10 from a minority ethnic background.

Ramesh is today the Global Ambassador for a major global law firm in Ince, a company that does value his approach as they understand that Ramesh will invest in relationships and long-term relationships like few others. However, this is only one small part of the story as Ramesh gives much of his time to supporting young talent or in supporting charitable concerns. He is a man who gives much of himself as he knows that the more one engages in life and gives, the more one does get back. The richest lives are those led by those who give. Most people would have been satisfied with becoming a partner and enjoying the rewards that the role brings. However, Ramesh is motivated by a higher purpose—a belief that life is a privilege and something to be lived to the full. Success for Ramesh is not position or prestige, but a life lived to the maximum and with good intent.

Most will say that success comes with a price, and of course, there are compromises along the path. That is just the nature of the journey, but maybe the real judgment should be the character that emerges at the other end. Ramesh is a fierce and loyal friend with a love of life and people. Lawyers would have a far stronger reputation if more acted in the manner that Ramesh has done over the years.

Over the years, he has raised, both directly and indirectly, over two million pounds for various charities, including the Cancer Relief Macmillan Fund and Anti-Slavery International, among others. In recognition of his social and charity work, Ramesh was appointed an officer of the Order of the British Empire (OBE) in the New Year's Honors List for 2001.

To provide an insight into the man, it may be best to hear his own words. He is quoted as saying:

"There is an old proverb used in the villages of Russia that says – 'Eyes scare but hands do,' so stop worrying about things and simply start doing. 'Follow your passion and live your dream.' Success does not always come easily and there is no substitute for hard work. My concern is that too many young people follow fashion rather than passion and this leads to so many of them dropping out after organisations have invested a lot of money in training them. Even worse, so many of them end up suffering from depression, anxiety and stress."

Ramesh has met many of the great figures across the world, including Her Majesty The Queen, Prince Charles, Princess Anne, Archbishop Desmond Tutu, and other world leaders. However, the day that Ramesh will most talk about is the time that he spent with Mother Teresa. Ramesh had encouraged clients of his to build an orphanage for Mother's charity in Calcutta and was invited to be at the handover ceremony. Her humility and dedication left a lasting impression on Ramesh. He watched first-hand how she interacted with the children and the stresses and strains that she endured in life.

Maybe this is what marks Ramesh out as being different. Yes, he followed his passion. Yes, he enjoyed success and recognition, but he has as much thirst to learn today as he did over the years ago when he first dreamed of becoming a lawyer. He will want to listen and learn from everyone he meets, and it is this *inner humility and passion* that give him a very genuine authenticity and passion for life.

Ramesh Vala

PART VI

What Lies Next?

CHAPTER 14

The Test of Character that Can Make a Difference

There will be few found, leaders who have been in role for a good length of tenure, who will regret either having been a leader or the lessons that they will have learned along their own journeys. They will possess scars, often deep ones. They will have endured some dark moments, and at times, the role will have felt highly painful and pointless. However, they still will look at their tenure with some pride. They will feel that they were privileged to have had the opportunity to make a difference, regardless of whether they may have failed or have been lauded for their success. All know that success and failure are remarkably close companions. It is all about a matter of small margins, and it is the small margins that ultimately make the difference.

Sir Clive Woodward (126), the former England Rugby Union Coach who led England to glory at the Rugby World Cup of 2003, often talked about the small margins that determine success. He would note that the difference between a great team and a good team, who would win nothing, was less than 2 percent. He would focus his players on improving 1 percent at a time, and if they could improve by 10 percent, the chances are that they would be world-class players. The more world-class players a team possessed, the better the odds. The more confidence the players possessed, the more leaders emerged across the team and the stronger the whole unit became. It was a simple and yet highly effective philosophy.

John McEnroe, one of the great tennis players and World Number 1 of the early 1980s, would often make a very similar point that there was very little difference in the skill levels of the top 100 players in the world; the differential lay in the mental approach of the player. Could a player mentally handle the big moments in the game—the pressure moments?

Does a player have the inner belief that they could win? Or, would doubts surface, which undermine performance?

> So, much of success in leadership is about the mental ability of a person to absorb pressure, be calm, and find solutions. It does take time to learn and few are able to achieve it; for it does need, within each person, a motivating factor to ensure that the leader accepts the bad moments and learns so that they can improve.

It is no surprise that so many dyslexics have achieved the highest honors across so many fields—politics, sport, acting, film, business, and science. Far more will have failed and fallen short. For those who did succeed, they accepted their shortcomings and found their own solutions. It will have been a painful journey, but they found new solutions to how they could fulfill their dreams. Today, dyslexia is understood to a far greater level, but there are lessons still for many corporates to learn because, if only 1 percent of talent within corporates are dyslexic, then are those companies missing out on a major talent pool?

It is also no surprise that so many dyslexics found their home in hospitality. For a long period of time, hospitality has been an industry that has been perceived as almost a second-class profession. Just like many dyslexics, the industry has so often been slighted, felt inferior to others, but just simply ploughed on. Only today is it beginning to realize the real scale and scope of its potential.

Hospitality today is viewed by many professionals across all the great disciplines as one of the most exciting industry sectors. Hotels, restaurants, stadia catering, food service, and bars are seen to be exciting environments and businesses that many venture capitalists and investors today want to invest in. It used to be viewed as a highly risky investment. Today, there is the utmost respect for the business leadership that the sector has displayed over the last three decades.

However, there is more to come. Hospitality can be a leading force in society, in communities, in those that it employs, and it can be a role model for other industries to follow. Hospitality has traveled a long and hard road, but today, it is a truly world-class industry, with world-class talent in a whole range of disciplines from management to the culinary:

from reception to housekeeping, from restaurants to bars to major events. There is an exciting new era awaiting to see the industry take the small leap up to the next level.

This is not to hide from the number of challenges that the industry does still face. There is a need for a stronger relationship between industry and education beyond the top hotel schools that have long dominated the landscape. A world-class industry needs a world-class structure and system to support the development of the young. It needs to be progressive and to find a stronger voice. For this, it needs investment. Education needs to make the argument, and industry needs to work far more closely in support.

It is the same in relation to talent. Investment in learning and development has fallen over the last 20 years. It needs to be reinvested in, as training is vital to any world-class industry. For too long, the industry has relied for the natural skills and resources of the people it employs. They go almost the extra mile as a rule, but excellence comes through training and, of course, through great leadership, which inspires a desire for excellence.

Leadership does still sit at the heart of it all. This is also where the greatest challenges for long-term success sit. There is a major need to build real trust back between leader, the board, and employees. It is a three-dimensional problem and takes the first two, the leader and board, to work far better and closer together in order to achieve success. There needs to be a re-focus on values, culture, internal communication, and giving people a real voice one that is actively promoted, actually appreciated, and listened to.

Companies need to rediscover how they can once again free up talent, to be brave, to be vocal, and to take risk. All the research tells us this is where the core faults lie, and there needs to be new strategies generated to combat the barriers that have been put in place.

There is very little evidence to support the notion that appointing good young talent into leadership roles is riskier than appointing experienced, older people. There is a lot of evidence that does suggests that experience and competence can sometimes be detrimental. It is natural that experienced leadership becomes defensive, conservative, and protective in approach. Sometimes, leadership needs a touch of the naïve. It can make a major difference.

Many of greatest U.S. presidents were all aged under 60 when they left office; Abraham Lincoln was 56 when he was fatally shot. JFK in his 40s. Clinton was in his 50s when he left office, Obama too.

Leadership is about inspiring others. For this to be achieved, a vision needs to be set; a dream even. People want to follow another. They want to be led, but, so many today talk openly of feeling starved of leadership that they feel they have confidence in.

The challenge that lies ahead is a mix of setting a vision, an objective that others feel that they want to follow. It must be their choice where they will want to improve their skills and will work hard to improve by those small 1 percent margins, and in setting an environment where people feel safe and can put their trust in leadership.

It is not an easy mission, but it is one that is worth the fight to try and achieve. It is a privilege and a responsibility to shoulder, and it can be deeply rewarding, both financially, but far more in the pride that it makes one feel.

It is time for a new, broader philosophy to emerge in hospitality, one that takes the industry forward and builds on the strong legacy that has been built to date.

Appendix

Published Articles

A modern dilemma. There is an argument to empower the twenty-somethings (Gen Z) over Gen X and Gen Y. They possess the motivation to make a difference. Can business empower them?
Published by EP magazine, 31st May 2020

As planning for a return to work steps up in earnest, there are a number of interesting discussions which have been circling. We, as with many others, regularly talk of the difference between generations and it may be that this will be become even obvious in the times to come but maybe not as many would expect.

For too long company leadership teams have been concerned about the lack of emerging leaders break through. The baby boomers have been held to blame but of course, the situation is not so simplistic. However it may be that now the baby boom generation could find a natural "ally" in those aged in their early twenties (Gen Z) and this naturally will create some key tensions. Gen Z it is argued are educated, motivated and determined to a level not seen since the baby boomers came to work.

Some Background

- There are some tensions emerging between those companies who do wish to see their people return to the office and those who are planning for their teams to work from home. Research indicates that that only 25% have a desire to return to the office for a traditional 5 day week. From now on, many will seek a new balance between home work and the office. This is probably inevitable and the traditionalists who do argue for the office will need to compromise.
- On the BBC yesterday, there was a discussion over software which many companies can and are downloading which

will measure an employee's productivity whilst working at home. It allows managers to continue to manage productivity and ensure that work is being done. It measures work taking place on a laptop. However, the counter is that is does show a lack of trust, is intrusive and does not measure thinking time.

- It may be that bigger issue is the lack of trust that the implementation of such software does suggest. Lack of trust has become a major talking point over the last few years. So too has a decline in productivity and the irony of course is that many companies started the year wanting to see a reduction in home working as the evidence was that it was not as effective as had been hoped. Given that many companies wanted to see more of their people in offices, one can understand the implementation of software such as the above bar it may well cause more issues than it solves.

- Traditionalists also argue that the millennials have been poor to network and that networking is key in this time to building trust with clients, with colleagues and in learning. More is learnt from informal comms. It is felt that there has been a decline in knowledge shown by millennials compared to previous generations and that it is important that the bar is raised. Millennials will, of course, counter by noting that in real terms L&D has declined quite dramatically. They will also note that there is a lack of trust in the behaviours of business leaders and not enough on real issues of environment, sustainability and social support which are important to this rising generation.

So where does the issue go from here?

- There is a lot of evidence emerging that the early twentysomethings (Gen Z) are a very different breed to those in their thirties and forties (Gen X and Gen Y). Gen X began work in a boom period and at the start of a technological revolution. They found promotion and advancement during the boom period relatively easy and have lived arguably in the safest economic period on record. Many point to these factors for the lack of real new leaders emerging through as with previous generations as the base hunger and motivation had been diluted. Is this fair? It is certainly fair to argue that the baby boom generation evolved in a far harder world so there would be a natural difference.

- For the twentysomethings the picture is very different as they have were the generation to leave university with real debt levels and now found the ground almost taken from beneath them as they begin to build their careers and some hope of buying property. They have had to work harder and have been under more pressure and scrutiny than almost any previous generation. There is an argument emerging that whatever the issues, right or wrong, with the Gen X, the twentysomethings are a generation worth investing in, and empowering. They have the hunger and energy to make a difference and they really want to see those above move aside.

- Many in Gen Z have commented that they have found weak mentors and managers in their Gen X/Y superiors. Their concern is that Gen X/Y could well be barriers to the progress of Gen Z.

- There is a natural friction which is emerging and which businesses need to be aware of and plan for. There is a distrust between the baby boom and Gen X for reasons which have been well accounted for: and then again between Gen X , Gen Y and Gen Z

Confused?

The real point is that many experts believe that we are seeing the emergence of a new generation who have real leadership potential and can lead a shift in business environments. It can be their motivation, intellect and energy that can lead a path through the crisis.

Are companies ready to innovate with new thinking in order to engage far, far better?

Published June, 2020 by EP Business in Hospitality

One of the most common conversations with senior Industry figures in recent weeks has been a genuine, heartfelt concern over the futures that many under the aged of 30 face. They are directly in the firing line and yet this emerging generation is one of the brightest, arguably one of the most naturally skilled for the new world to come and has the energy which will be needed as the rebuilding process begins.

However are companies ready to engage this generation with new ideas, new thinking and support?

The concern is that most are not close to being ready for what will be needed. The last 3 months have shed a new light on a number of factors:

- There is a genuine concern over how it is the youngest in workplaces who seem to be the most vulnerable. Companies seemed to have protected than senior players over the more junior and this has sent out a message within companies as to how a company values its people. It is estimated that close to 1:4 under 25 will lose their jobs and maybe 1:3. It will though those at the front end and the younger talent that companies will need once life does return, so has the approach of the last few months been the right one? How will companies engage the young again?
- It is those aged under 25 that today carry large burdens in terms of debt, so there is a need for companies to maybe do more to be supportive of this group.
- It has been noted that the loudest voices in the crisis are still those aged over 55. Where are the 35-45 old year leaders who have long been the ones with energy to create change? They exist but their voices are not being heard. They need to be
- During the crisis, one can argue it has been the senior players who have kept things ticking over but often the lowest paid parts of society. – Delivery staff, cleaners, security, shopkeepers let alone nurses and caterers.

- Will HR change? HR has been a common area of great debate over the last decade: mainly as its role has changed over the years. In the 1980s and 90s, HR was an important part of a business and rightly sat at the board table. It would champion the importance of people and strong cultures. In the early 00s there was a shift to becoming more about cost control, process and protecting shareholder return. The role of HR simply mirrored the changes in business and economics. Now is the opportunity for that all to change as little will be more important than how talent and people are engaged post the Covid crisis.

The irony of course is that there are many positives taking place. These positives do shine a light potentially on the gap in how many companies are thinking. The question is whether these are being recognised within company strategies?

- There has been a whole campaign of work to help the vulnerable and feed the most needy.
- Society has come together in a way not see since the 1940s.
- There is a real energy for being creative and innovative amongst the young. They know they face a challenge but they are staying positive. They lack trust that their employers will retain them so they are preparing new ideas. This energy will be needed.
- The same is true with students. They have maintained their belief and desire to build careers and have adapted. Has Industry spoken to them as effectively as it could?
- People have worked from home as effectively as they can during this period.
- Research has already suggested that more will be invested in sustainability.
- There is also a call for more genuine and authentic behaviours.

This all together provides a time to start again in how we manage people—and it is important. Feedback from forum after forum is suggesting that:

- Service will be a key differential as we rebuild
- Younger employees will not accept poor leadership behaviours. They do expect the bar to be raised.
- History has shown that the young often create the entrepreneurial spirit to create real change
- There is a real desire for more progressive thinking and strategies re diversity and inclusion. Many of the existing stats are simply seen as not good enough
- Research has indicated that pre the crisis that only 13% were positively engaged in their work and that over 34 days per year were lost in sick days and presenteeism. 75% of those aged under 35 do not want to return to office environment as they once were. Yet only 17% want to work from home.
- Leaders will be forced to communicate in a very different way.
- The Deloittes report on Millennials in 2019 noted that the majority did not feel that business was run on ethical grounds and want to see a broad business-society collaboration as seen during lockdown.

So are companies ready to engage those that may have been most alienated during the crisis but will be needed now? Are companies ready to engage new thinking, strategies and innovation to support those that will matter most?

It will need careful thought and planning. How ready are you?
It maybe that many look back at this time as the catalyst for positive change, when we once again placed human capita at the core of business but allied with innovative AI. At last we find a strong balance. Maybe we all the raise the bar in how we collaborate and work together?

"Whenever one is on the side of the majority, it is time to pause and reflect" (Mark Twain)
Published by EP Business in Hospitality, June 2020

Are you happy to stand alone when others disagree with you? Few are able to do this. This has always been the case but the strength to do so, starts with learning to socialise, network and be communicate effectively. It is a skill which has marked out leaders for many years. It is a skill which comes with time and experience for it is not easy to stand apart.

The learning place for this skill has long laid in networking and social conversation. It is said that networking has become a lost art and yet some of the best and most important learning comes from networking, from informal discussion and debate. If networking is a lost art, then the danger is that conversation will be too – and that would be a sad state of affairs.

Is it a coincidence that many complain of less knowledge if networking is not promoted? It is so important to test one's knowledge through conversation and through building a broader network. As we start to enter a world of less opportunity, the more it will be essential that networking is promoted as a skill & art form.

Part of building trust and confidence is by being visible and accessible to audiences. Networking is a key part of building confidence and ensuring that relationships are in place. In simplistic terms it is about the ability to access knowledge, support, help and open doors when it matters.

In these most challenging of times, we surely would like to see emerging leaders that are out there, clear, visible and accessible as this builds confidence. One may not agree with them, but it does also build behaviours. Its builds strength in others. It can start with networking and with having the confidence to disagree with others, to stand alone when it matters.

Hospitality playing a role in society
"Proud to be supporting both the Country and the NHS"
Published by EP, Business in Hospitality on 25th April 2020.
The NEC is one of the primary sites for the new Nightingale Hospitals that have been founded to combat Covid-19. EP spoke to the Amadeus team central to supporting this effort.

There are many hospitality operators who are sitting in lockdown, frustrated and wondering as to what the future may hold. For others, they have found their lives almost turned upside down or suddenly changed in outlook and daily work patterns. Such an example is the award-winning food service company, Amadeus, who have seen themselves one month hosting vibrant concerts, dinners and exhibitions and the next working closely with Public Health England, the NHS, fellow NEC Group colleagues and the military to open a major facility to combat Covid-19.

For many of us, Covid-19 is still all a touch surreal as we sit in lockdown relatively safe and secure. For those who are turning such major spaces into special healthcare operations, it all becomes far closer to a very real and serious reality. Last Thursday a new 500 bed facility was opened at the NEC. Amadeus was brought on board as the nominated caterer to look after not only the F&B requirements for workers on site during build, but to support on designing staff rooms/canteens and menus for any incoming frontline staff and patients.

EP was, therefore, keen to talk to the operational team and hear their views as to how it has impacted on their lives and how they believe it will change their behaviours post crisis.

One very clear message came across consistently from the interviews which was the genuine pride that the team has had in making a contribution during the crisis.

Paul Bate, the Operations Director commented:

It is a fresh experience for all of us. The biggest challenge has been figuring out the processes to keep people safe during this time—our first and biggest priority. However, everyone has been brilliant. They see that they have an opportunity to make a real difference for both the country and for the NHS and they have embraced the challenge.

Annie Monnox, General Manager agreed;

Our team has been superb. They just want to help and this situation has shown hospitality employees at their best. It has been lovely to see and is a testament to our team.

Our challenge is to make sure everyone is kept as safe as can be. We are specialists in running events and in many ways, this is another event – just a different layout and challenge. It is one though that no one thought we would be involved in but it is, and we just want to make sure that we do the best that we can. The Amadeus team has been excellent in making sure that we all have had the right PPE, that we are fully equipped and supported.

Kane Bridgeman, General Manager at the NEC also concurred:

Everyone is proud to be working on the project and it has been a real experience, if only it were under better circumstances.

We always have the ability to deliver; we are experienced in adapting to different events. Another challenge was working to such a short timescale from concept to delivery. Everything has moved at such speed. I think it is fair to say that we have all been learning as we go, but the feedback from those that we have been working with – such as Public Health England – has been very good.

So what have been the main challenges faced in mobilising and preparing the facility from an Amadeus perspective?

Marc Frankl, F&B Director noted;

One of the things that many operators agree on is that as we come out of this crisis, our view of food waste will be different. Prior to lockdown, we were carrying a lot of stock so we have been working on the best methods to maximise the use of this and also make sure that our food has been excellent and nutritional for all workers on site. We have also been working closely with suppliers to make sure that they feel supported and are able to meet our needs. It has been very hard on them and they need to know that we are there for them. It is about partnership and collaboration.

The biggest challenge though undoubtedly has been in preparing all the additional safety measures but has provided great learning; we've tested ideas in a tough environment.

Paul Bate made the same observation; "We have tested new operational procedures that we know work and will benefit us in the long-term."

Will their behaviours change as we emerge from the crisis?

"We will have learnt more about how to deliver safely," noted Marc Frankl. "We are now working on new innovation for when we return to business as usual and start to host events again. We are looking at 'self-serve' beer systems, screen between tables and new service techniques."

People are more respectful of each other's space. I also see a kinder, more compassionate approach to social interaction within the team and on the streets and I hope that this stays. I think most people want it to.

observed Kane Bridgman.

Annie Monnox made a different point:

I would hope we all learn something from this time. More of us are buying from local shops and suppliers. The local shops have been outstanding and this will not be forgotten.

Our senior team is also now working on blue sky thinking for the future and this is fascinating to be part of. They have shown themselves to be a great group to work with – positive, understanding and wanting to make a difference.

In all the interviews with the Amadeus team, it was clear that the individuals had really taken on the challenge of catering for this facility, and took positive learnings from a job they wish they never had to do. It is important to note, that although hospitality has been badly affected by the crisis, there are many people across the country who have wanted to step forward and make a difference in spite of the personal pressures that they have been facing.

Kevin Watson, Managing Director of Amadeus, commented:

I am very proud of what the team is achieving at this most difficult time – but what has made this a really special time, is also the hundreds of hand drawn pictures or rainbows that have been sent in from the children on team members. This has been a very rare time when it has not just been the team that have put themselves out but also their families. It is humbling to watch just how communities have once again placed others first.

The Amadeus team is reflective of the many in the industry, and one can sense both their pride to play an active role but also their determination to continue delivering excellent service for all

This does need to be resolved.
400,000 children under 16 years of age face food insecurity in London. Over half do not qualify for government food vouchers during the Covid-19 crisis published by EP Business in Hospitality on April 15, 2020 (64)

It almost sounds like it should be a story from a Dicken's novel, reflecting poverty in the Victorian years of the 1800s – but sadly, it is the harsh truth that many children are facing today, currently isolated, at risk of hunger and scared for the future.

Surely this needs to not allowed so the question does need to be asked—can we work together to create meaningful change that does move this situation on?

Kitchen Social is a Mayor's Fund for London working with local community organizations to feed and support children across the Capital. Clara Widdowson, a project lead for Kitchen Social, reached out to Thomas Franks in recent weeks in order to gain support. The Thomas Franks Foundation – the charitable arm of Thomas Franks—generously supported by Barings, are now providing meals across six Kitchen Social hubs—in Barnet, Ealing, Greenwich, Lambeth, Southwark and Tower Hamlets.

It is a good story of the moment but more needs to be done. The Food Service sector has really stepped forward during this crisis and made a major difference when it has mattered. However, this situation does need to be resolved once and for all. Can the sector work together to solve this issue for today and for the future?

On Tuesday, The Trustees of the Thomas Franks Foundation met and decided that they would work to try and lead this change through their charitable arm. They will applying for grants and funding. However, it is also important that business also comes together to support such an important initiative.

As we learn lessons from this crisis, the question is asked – should nurses in future be fed for free?

From Boris Johnson to thousands of others, there are cries of appreciation for the courage and care shown by Nurses in the NHS. We all know that nurses are not well paid but believe in something that is bigger than themselves. One question that is now being posed is whether Nurses should, in future, expect to gain greater benefits from an appreciative society?

Over the last few weeks, there have been a number of heart-warming stories emerge over a range of companies that become involved in supporting the NHS. At the same time, there have been a number of consultants that have written in asking the question – will these companies still be there once this crisis is past?

However, maybe the real question should be is – how will we change post crisis and make sure that those that have led the battle against the crisis be better supported in the future?

Isn't this all a cry for genuine change?

Industry Collaboration

Thomas Franks and Compass are already now collaborating together. As of later this week, Thomas Franks will be working with Compass at the Excel London Nightingale Hospital to provide 4000 chilled meals for nurses and doctors to take home. It takes the pressure off the real heroes in this crisis and gives them the support they desire and it is a great example of the Industry working together.

The Thomas Franks Foundation

One can be, of course, cynical but the Thomas Franks Foundation wants to make a difference to both the above issues. It wants to do its part in feeding children, doctors and nurses for today and for the long term. Of course this needs support and it is important that we do start to put away the traditional petty rivalries to do something that places these groups first and makes sure we can all contribute to meaningful change.

How does it make people feel to contribute?
We asked the team at Thomas Franks how they felt to work for no reward and to contribute during the Coronavirus lockdown. These were some of the comments:

> Thomas Franks have given me so many opportunities, Thomas Franks feeding communities has given me the opportunity to give back

Gavin Tarbox (Development Chef)

> Everyday I work alongside driven, passionate, successful people... but in these less fortunate times it's clear they genuinely care about those they work with and the community in which they live... chefs hats off to you all

Thomas Cuthbert
Regional Development Chef

> It's great to be part of the TF family, working for a company who shares my passion for fresh food and food innovation.
> Also Proud to be part of the TF family who in these difficult and challenging times are supporting our amazing NHS by providing fresh nutritional meals to key workers.

Fraser Ross
Development Chef

> As a foodie it's been really inspirational and has been wonderful to give back at a time when so many are suffering amazing to see so many giving totally inspired, we are such a beautiful warming company with an incredible founder so so inspirational.
> I'm so glad I'm involved never felt like this before thank you Thomas franks

Stuart Howard
Regional Development Chef

> To be able to be involved with the Thomas Franks Feeding
> Communities project is what Thomas Franks is all about "being
> involved" as an independent caterer using local suppliers we are
> able to act immediately when required supporting local suppliers
> and feeding a whole community .
>
> This gives myself and my team a feeling of belonging, making
> us feel proud to be key workers on behalf of Thomas Franks

Dean Collins
Catering Manager Rendcomb College

> As Catering Manager working within Thomas Franks, I am proud
> to be apart of our company's efforts to raze funds and help feed
> our communities, with the support of St Leonards school in fife
> Scotland and our suppliers we can now give something back and
> do or part in supplying healthy nutritious meals to the most vul-
> nerable people in their time of need.

Darren Tonge
Catering Manager

> I'm excited to be able to help give back to those who are less fortu-
> nate than we are, Thomas Franks and Westholme school working
> together to support the Blackburn with Darren area in its time of
> need. Its encouraging to work for a company that is so committed
> to their staff and the places they work in these unprecedented times.

James Pate,Catering Manager

**St.John's create twin strategies to care for students and the vulnerable
Article published by EP on 30th April 2020**
For the past few weeks, we have proudly been writing about and sharing
inspirational stories of food service operators providing food solutions to

and catering for vulnerable people within their communities during this most trying of times. The pride felt by operators and their employees by being able to truly help where they are most needed whilst still putting themselves at risk has been heart warming and greatly appreciated. Many operators have in doing so also helped support suppliers and made the most of their operational infrastructure despite the lockdown.

St John's College of the University of Cambridge have too welcomed the challenge of caring for those most vulnerable in their local community, as well as embracing very innovative thinking, all whilst still being operational.

With many students and fellows still in residence, St John's have had to adapt their offer and their operation at speed whilst still ensuring that all under their care have been catered for during this time of isolation and lockdown. This did not detract from their desire to use their facilities and supply chain to help those vulnerable in care homes within Cambridge.

Bill Brogan, Catering and Conference Manager at St John's College proudly confirmed that the college has been, in addition to providing normal on site catering, providing additional catering support to two care homes within Cambridge being the Orchard House Care Home and Great Shelford Care Home. Freshly prepared portions are individually boxed and accompanied with an allergy card and delivered to the homes by St John's catering staff. This additional support has really boosted staff morale and wellbeing as well as having helped the college support their suppliers, as orders have increased from the norm to provide for this additional catering.

Plans to invite the staff from the two venues for a lovely afternoon tea at the College in the Autumn when life returns to normal are already in motion.

In addition to the above, college chefs recently received new chefs uniforms which meant that the old ones would simply be collected and disposed. This was until, and in line with their entrepreneurial spirit, that the college found a company in Suffolk who is now re-appropriating the uniforms and turning them into face masks to help support those vulnerable and on the front line.

There really are opportunities to support and innovate everywhere, it just takes the will, the entrepreneurial spirit and the selflessness to create partnerships for the best outcomes for all.

Leadership

Traditional messages do not get heard. As a new generational rises in importance, it is important to change the message.

- **Published by EP Business In Hospitality on May 24, 2020**

The years of leadership by the Baby Boom generation is coming to its natural conclusion. It will inevitably result in a shift from the one of the most successful business generations ever to the millennials generation: a generation which is unproven, untested and yet are an exciting prospect as they are progressive, socially and environmentally aware, diverse and aspiring to see a better world. Both generations should work together to ease the way but the chasm between the generations is arguably too large to achieve this.

With all the statistics which have been reported, it is clear that there is a gulf between the traditional methodologies and the perspective possessed by millennials. It is easy to see how many times both media and political commenters have been inaccurate in recent years. Their understanding has been based on the traditional and they have misunderstood how often external audiences have been disengaged from their messages. How many times have we all been shocked by political results in recent times? Just consider the Brexit result, The US Election and the UK General Election. There is good reason why this does happen.

It has been very clear during Lockdown that so many of the Industry forums have been still dominated by the same voices. Fair enough but there has been an absence of those aged under 40. It is not that they are not welcome; it is more that they have not engaged.

It is the same within companies when leadership teams are often still following a traditional doctrine with little true understanding that their messages and processes simply do not engage. As one understands this point, it is easy to then understand why there is such a chasm between the generations. The reported levels of disengagement has been ignored time and again. Little has been done to understand the social changes which have taken place.

One needs to remember that the Baby Boomers grew up in harder times. The 1970s were not an easy time and respect for one's senior was central within work and social culture. Leadership was far more dictatorial and the word of the leader was deemed as final. That is simply no longer the case with a modern society which will question everything. The processes and approaches of old no longer work. The central messages no longer resonate.

Leadership teams do need to adapt their thinking and approaches for the new generation which is emerging. The only place to start with stronger engagement and the building of greater trust.

Many will argue that the starting place for change begins at board level as, at times, these have been less than properly functional. There is certainly evidence that many boards have been less than united in objective. This is natural for the pressure on a board would only have increased as the greater the chasm developed between generations. The task is now to come together and be more effective if culture is to be strong and trust rebuilt.

This process starts with engaging and listening far better than has been the case.

We'll work hard so that we can meet again.

• **Published by EP Business in Hospitality on May 16, 2020**

A senior industry player last week spoke of his pain in having to make redundancies. Although the Furlough scheme remains in place, he wanted to stay the rebuilding process early. His message to those he cut was "We do care about you. We want to work with you again so we will work hard now so that we can meet again."

Afterwards he talked of his reasoning:

I was....I am....frustrated with how industry leaders have said so little about our people. We need to show compassion, so I felt it was right to be upfront and tell them early what the truth is. They knew the truth and the feedback that I have had is that they have respected the way we have gone about it. We have said that in any new job opening, one of those being redundant will have preference if they want to re-join. We are a family. It is my duty to them that we will work as hard as we can so that we can re-employ as many as we can as soon as we can.

Why I am frustrated by others? Those furloughed deserve to be treated with respect and with compassion. They are waiting on us, on our actions and it must be a tough place to be. I have prided myself throughout my life that I have relied only on me.....but this crisis would have taken that away from me and I would have had no option but to rely on others. Horrible place to be.

My hope is that as an industry we do see real compassion and care for those that lose their jobs. I know the estimates are beyond 300,000, maybe 400,000 and we need to stand together – those who have lost their jobs and employers who can in time re-employ them.

I absolutely believe this is the right message for this time and the right way that we should behave.

"You don't get talent readymade – you need to work with them. We need to talk to them – not leave them waiting for us to act"

- **Published by EP Business in Hospitality on May 3, 2020**

These are the words of one of the UK's leading hoteliers who was talking about the need for leaders to send out some positive messages to younger talent at a time when many – especially those about to graduate and enter the industry – must be wondering about their future careers.

In fairness, there will be many across all ages and all levels who will be wondering about their careers. There is a genuine need for Industry leaders to make some positive statements about the future and how the industry will need all that want to help it rebuild.

It has become a discussion piece which is growing in volume. At a virtual discussion which EP hosted on Friday last week, one leading hotelier noted;

> I am surprised by the lack of commentary being offered by leaders. It is part of leadership to reassure teams and people and I am seeing very little reassurance being offered anywhere. I know it is difficult but it is part of the job. Whatever happens we are going to need young people who want to develop careers in the sector—so we need to surely be saying something to those wanting to enter the Industry.

We have written a number of articles about a growing desire by many for a stronger social agenda to emerge post crisis where companies do work better together to support community and social causes. However, for this is secondary to the need for companies to place the talent and people piece back at the heart of the board agenda – not just in word but also in action. Many have commented how they are bored of the great words spoken re talent development – that there will be little tolerance afterwards for great words and little action of substance. We will need to rebuild with solid pillars.

Returning the leading hotelier who spoke the words in the title:

> I know a number of hotels who are starting to talk about making young talent redundant as they can be easily replaced. We can be arrogant can't we? Same theme. You don't get talent that is ready made. It needs to be developed. It needs to be motivated by the companies. I do get bored at companies criticising the many great young people around, who often want to do well. Companies want this talent to be better with no training. Well we were trained. We were invested in so why do we think it is different today?

Strong words but these words are being spoken in greater numbers. If the Industry is going to rebuild, it will need to do so with the young as well as the experienced. They will need to know that they matter. In the

1990s, there were numerous reports published which highlighted that training and development was the primary reason why a person stayed with a company and what attracted the best talent. Research will not show this today as so many lack faith in how companies are committed to development. Many expect this to see genuine change as times and rebuilding moves on.

Hospitality Skills are a premium today. It needs believing in and investing in with no excuses.

- **Published by EP Business in Hospitality on March 6, 2020**

It never ceases to amaze me how seriously and respectfully that those outside of the Hospitality Industry view it – but those within it still struggle to understand that it is a business that not only excites interest, it has skilled world-class practitioners who have a much desired skill set.

Business sectors from banking to law to financial services like to recruit from hospitality skills. They don't see hospitality schools as the poor relation to many management and business schools so why do we?

A true hospitality skill set is of such importance and should be valued more highly.

The Industry is world class and it does need a hotel school that can support it well. Not just any hotel school but one which is truly progressive, in tune with the young and with industry and that can really help nurture younger talent. The Swiss Hotel School have correctly led the way and they have developed a well-deserved reputation for excellence. The UK should be wanting to compete with this; to create as school that is fit for purpose for the 21st Century Industry. The Edge Hotel School is a great example but more is needed. There are many great educators in the system but the system needs evolution.

Regardless of whether one agrees with the above or not, the truth is that hospitality is one of the leading industries in the UK, is world-class and needs a strong support framework that nurtures young talent.

As an industry we should be striving to create centres of excellence in the key disciplines to really engage and develop the skills of the young. We should be getting back into schools, making sure that the young are trained not just in cooking but in their social skills. Strong social competence and the ability to be a visible leaders are two of the most important skills in life – regardless of industry.

There many reasons why this does not happen but instead, we need to find answers for why it can happen.

References

1. Brainy Quote www.brainyquote.com - https://brainyquote.com/quotes/winston_churchill_124653
2. The Kipling Society. Rudyard Kipling and his poem "If" http://kiplingsociety.co.uk/poems_if.htm
3. Brainy Quote www.brainyquote.com - https://brainyquote.com/quotes/warren_bennis_121715
4. EPInsights – www.epinsights.co.uk
   a. Brainy Quote - https://www.brainyquote.com/quotes/mark_twain_122378
5. The JFK Presidential Library https://jfklibrary.org/learn/education/teachers/curricular-resources/elementary-school-curricular-resources/ask-not-what-your-country-can-do-for-you
6. Wikipedia https://en.wikipedia.org/wiki/Neville_Chamberlain
7. Quote Investigator - https://quoteinvestigator.com/2014/06/28/success/
8. EP Insights – www.epinsights.co.uk - Published by EP Insights May 14th 2020
9. Simon Thomas 4th May 2020 Wales Online https://walesonline.co.uk/sport/rugby/rugby-news/no-dickheads-allowed-blacks-mental-12986818
10. NZ Herald 20th April 2020 https://nzherald.co.nz/sport/news/article.cfm?c_id=4&objectid=12325932
11. EP Insights. Research by EP Insights
12. The Guardian. 5th Jan 2017. By Philip Inman https://theguardian.com/business/2017/jan/05/chief-economist-of-bank-of-england-admits-errors
13. The World at Work 22 Jan 20202 https://worldatwork.org/workspan/articles/average-age-for-c-suite-member-is-56.
14. Focus Adventure. Article by Leonrad Kok http://focusadventure.com/team-building/gallery/the-emotional-bank-account/
15. 311 Institute. Article by Matthew Griffin 13th May 2017 https://311institute.com/experts-are-starting-to-agree-that-ai-will-replace-ceos/
16. The Economist. 6th May 2017. https:// economist.com/leaders/2017/05/06/the-worlds-most-valuable-resource-is-no-longer-oil-but-data
17. M. 28th April 2017 "Artificial Intelligence is the new electricity – Andrew Ng" https://medium.com/syncedreview/artificial-intelligence-is-the-new-electricity-andrew-ng-cc132ea6264
18. Wikipedia https://en.wikipedia.org/wiki/The_Current_War
19. Futurism. Christinna Reedy 28th April 2017. "Experts assert that AI will soon be replacing CEOs" https://futurism.com/experts-assert-that-ai-will-soon-be-replacing-ceos

20. Goodreads https://goodreads.com/quotes/2528-keep-away-from-people-who-try-to-belittle-your-ambitions

21. The Luxury Hotels of London 1991 by Chris Sheppardson

22. Goodreads https://goodreads.com/quotes/tag/social-status

23. Beqom https://beqom.com/blog/jfk-and-the-janitor

24. Forbes. Christine Comaford 28th Jan 2017. https://forbes.com/sites/christinecomaford/2017/01/28/63-of-employees-dont-trust-their-leader-heres-what-you-can-do-to-change-that/#221cb04a7de4

25. Vitality Healthiest Companies report https://vitality.co.uk/business/healthiest-workplace/findings/

26. Deloittes https://www2.deloitte.com/content/dam/Deloitte/global/Documents/About-Deloitte/deloitte-2019-millennial-survey.pdf

27. Wikipedia https://en.wikipedia.org/wiki/Big_Bang_(financial_markets)

28. The Guardian 26th April 2007 https://theguardian.com/politics/2007/apr/26/tonyblair.labour

29. Ecole Hotiere De Lausanne https://info.ehl.edu

30. Sophie Devonshire – "Superfast: Lead at Speed" https://books.google.co.uk/books?id=mvGnDgAAQBAJ&pg=PT6&lpg=PT6&dq=100+companies+in+the+FTSE+100+in+1984,+only+24+were+still+breathing+in+2012.&source=bl&ots=RMs27PsES_&sig=ACfU3U1PcwqM1CSLWMwS1rshAxlyWP9l2A&hl=en&sa=X&ved=2ahUKEwjX_oeiqYPpAhVmRRUIHb5qDe4Q6AEwAHoECAsQAQ#v=onepage&q=100%20companies%20in%20the%20FTSE%20100%20in%201984%2C%20only%2024%20were%20still%20breathing%20in%202012.&f=false

31. Deloittes https://www2.deloitte.com/content/dam/Deloitte/global/Documents/About-Deloitte/deloitte-2019-millennial-survey.pdf

32. BrainyQuote https://brainyquote.com/quotes/winston_churchill_165927

33. EPinsights www.epinsights.co.uk

34. EP Insights www.epinsights.co.uk

35. The Telegraph. 31st may 2009. Umree Kahn https://telegraph.co.uk/news/celebritynews/5416844/Gordon-Ramsay-admits-he-came-close-to-losing-his-business-empire.html

36. The Daily Mail 25th March 2020. Paul Thompson   https://dailymail.co.uk/news/article-8148839/Chef-slams-Gordon-Ramsay-terminates-employment-500-staff.html

37. The Sun. 20th April 2020. Stephanie Soteriou https://thesun.co.uk/tvandshowbiz/11438806/gordon-ramsay-cycles-miles/

38. The Sun. 7th April 2020 Stuart Pink https://thesun.co.uk/tvandshowbiz/11350446/gordon-ramsay-threatened-coronavirus-lockdown-cornwall-holiday-home/

39. The Daily Mail. 16th April 2020. Kate Thomas https://dailymail.co.uk/tvshowbiz/article-8224547/Gordon-Ramsay-continues-anger-Cornwall-residents-amid-coronavirus-lockdown.html

40. Imbd https://imdb.com/title/tt4606514/

41. The World Economic Forum 24th march 2015 https://weforum.org/agenda/2015/03/why-you-need-to-over-communicate/

42. Business Insider 16yh June 2018 Katie Canales - https://businessinsider.com/cafe-x-robotic-coffee-bar-automation-2018-6?r=US&IR=T#customers-can-use-on-site-kiosks-to-place-their-coffee-orders-3

43. Tech Crunch "Amazon opens its first grocery store" 2th febriary 2020. Sarah Perez. https://techcrunch.com/2020/02/25/amazon-opens-its-first-cashierless-grocery-store

44. Hotel Buddy https://hotel-buddy.de/?lang=en

45. BBC 29th August 2019 https://bbc.co.uk/news/technology-49508091

46. The Guardian 1st Feb 2016 https://theguardian.com/commentisfree/2016/feb/01/loneliness-at-work-introvert-sadness-bereft-in-bustling-office

47. New York Times. 17th January 2018 Ceylan Yeginsu https://nyti mes.com/2018/01/17/world/europe/uk-britain-loneliness.html

48. CV Library. Insights team 11th November 2019 https://cv-library.co.uk/recruitment-insight/brits-suffer-loneliness-workplace/

49. Forbes. 25th February 2020 Richard Eisenberg https://forbes.com/sites/nextavenue/2020/02/25/whos-lonely-at-work-and-why/#7edd51a27037

50. Wikipedia https://en.wikipedia.org/wiki/Barbarella_(film)

51. Wikipedia https://en.wikipedia.org/wiki/Sleeper_(1973_film)

52. Wikipedia https://en.wikipedia.org/wiki/Orgasmatron

53. Paro Robots http://www.parorobots.com/

54. Review 42. Denis Metev 4th July 2020 https://review42.com/how-much-time-do-people-spend-on-social-media/

55. The Independent 10th October 2019. Sabrina Barr https://independent.co.uk/life-style/health-and-families/social-media-mental-health-negative-effects-depression-anxiety-addiction-memory-a8307196.html

56. Inc. Geoffrey James https://inc.com/geoffrey-james/the-average-worker-spends-51-of-each-workday-on-these-3-unnecessary-tasks.html

57. New York Intelligencer. 6th Dec 2019 . Andrew Sullivan http://nymag.com/intelligencer/2019/12/boris-johnson-brexit.html

58. Forbes. 9th December 2019 Jack McCullough https://forbes.com/sites/jackmccullough/2019/12/09/the-psychopathic-ceo/#7f84fa7791e3

59. Forbes 9th December 2019. Jack McCullough https://forbes.com/sites/jackmccullough/2019/12/09/the-psychopathic-ceo/#7bb4bac3791e

60. FT.Com. February 24th 2013. Tim Faley and Peter Adriaens. "Scools do think too narrowly on entrepreneurship" https://ft.com/content/483c4068-6a3e-11e2-a3db-00144feab49a

61. Wikipedia https://en.wikipedia.org/wiki/House_of_Commons_of_the_United_Kingdom

62. France 24–30th March 2020 https://france24.com/en/20200330-france-to-put-domestic-violence-victims-in-hotels-as-numbers-soar-under-coronavirus-lockdown

63. New York Times 17th December 2019. Alisha Haridasani Gupta https://nytimes.com/2019/12/17/us/california-boardroom-gender-quota.html

64. The Guardian. 4th December 2019. Philip Inman https://theguardian.com/business/2019/dec/04/top-uk-firms-failing-to-increase-boardroom-diversity-study-shows

65. McKinseys https://mckinsey.com/-/media/McKinsey/Business%20Functions/Organization/Our%20Insights/Delivering%20through%20diversity/Delivering-through-diversity_full-report.ashx

66. Deloittes https://deloitte.wsj.com/riskandcompliance/2019/03/12/women-and-minorities-on-fortune-500-boards-more-room-to-grow/

67. Peterson Institute International Economics February 2016 Marcus Noland (PIIE), Tyler Moran (PIIE) and Barbara Kotschwar (PIIE) https://piie.com/publications/working-papers/gender-diversity-profitable-evidence-global-survey

68. Price Waterhouse Coopers https://pwc.co.uk/industries/hospitality-leisure/women-in-hospitality-and-leisure.html)

69. Mckinseys https://mckinsey.com/business-functions/organization/our-insights/delivering-through-diversity

70. Deloittes https://www2.deloitte.com/content/dam/Deloitte/global/Documents/

71. Social talent www.socialtalent.com

72. Social Talent https://socialtalent.com/blog/recruitment/10-companies-around-the-world-that-are-embracing-diversity

73. Proctor & Gamble USA https://us.pg.com/gender-equality/

74. Healthline 20th December 2019 Mere Abrams https://healthline.com/health/different-genders.

75. BCG Henederson Institute. 23rd January 2018Rocío Lorenzo, Nicole Voigt, Miki Tsusaka, Matt Krentz, and Katie Abouzahr https://bcg.com/en-gb/publications/2018/how-diverse-leadership-teams-boost-innovation.aspx

76. Hays https://hays.com.sg/direport

77. Global Recruiter 21st November 2019 . Newsdesk https://theglobalrecruiter.com/creative-thinking-stifled-by-pressure-and-lack-of-leadership/

78. Global Recruiter. 21st November 2019. Newsdesk https://theglobalrecruiter.com/creative-thinking-stifled-by-pressure-and-lack-of-leadership/

79. Goodreads https://goodreads.com/quotes/523350-if-you-are-depressed-you-are-living-in-the-past

80. Wikipedia https://en.wikipedia.org/wiki/Impostor_syndrome

81. Ep Insights www.epinsights.co.uk

82. Vitality Healthiest Company Report https://vitality.co.uk/business/ healthiest-workplace/

83. Vitality Healthiest Company Report https://vitality.co.uk/business/ healthiest-workplace/

84. The Australian https://theaustralian.com.au/subscribe/news/1/?sourceCode =TAWEB_WRE170_a_GGL&dest=https%3A%2F%2Fwww. theaustralian.com.au%2Flife%2Fworkplace-stress-affects-73-per-cent-of-employees%2Fnews-story%2F2495662b85e6ef95ee5792f11b9c46ea&me mtype=anonymous&mode=premium

85. Personnel Today https://personneltoday.com/occupational-health-and-wellbeing/

86. The Huff Post 12th April 2013 https://huffpost.com/entry/work-stress-jobs-americans_n_3053428?guccounter=1&guce_referrer=aHR0cHM 6Ly93d3cuZ29vZ2xlLmNvbS88&guce_referrer_sig=AQAAAF eTTocxSFrLSdZZuGOzroDC3RLIwl84Kb8T9FCS88NsX5GL7xaS6O EpBvF6NcQxmTuWoE34cc3DHpmZNUHwJQ4zNI lCSBrIhTk7ZHsoYPybDy3an_QGy5bxGTPsZI92YdbshAGs_ CsJEBylopc1afgK9RUcxT0GPZqPWteapSb7

87. Anxiety and Depression Association America https://adaa.org/workplace-stress-anxiety-disorders-survey

88. Business Journals. Clifford Jones. 16th October 2017 https://https:// bizjournals.com/bizjournals/how-to/growth-strategies/2017/10/how-anxiety-hurts-workplace-productivity.html

89. FT. Com https://aboutus.ft.com/en-gb/new-agenda/

90. The Guardian 1st June 2010 . Tim Webb https://theguardian.com/ business/2010/jun/01/bp-response-oil-spill-tony-hayward

91. Smash the Box http://smashthebox.me/

92. Brainy Quote https://brainyquote.com/quotes/richie_benaud_308153

93. Twitter. 1st April 2020. YouGov https://twitter.com/yougov/status/1245395 321582235649?lang=en / https://telegraph.co.uk/news/politics/10137928/ Its-still-who-you-know-not-what-you-know-that-matters-say-two-thirds-of-Britons.html)

94. The Washington Post June 2019 https://washingtonpost.com/lifestyle/ 2019/06 /todays-parents-think-they-lack-time-or-skill-throw-dinner-parties-theyre-missing-out/.

95. Goodreads https://goodreads.com/quotes/389168-scrabble-was-invented-by-nazis-to-piss-off-kids-with

96. Goodreads https://goodreads.com/quotes/tag/dyslexia

97. Inc . Eric Markowitz 11th May 2011 https://inc.com/articles/201105/are-dyslexics-better-visionaries.html

98. Cass. "Dyslexia" Report by Julie Logan. 2009 https://cass.city.ac.uk/__data/assets/pdf_file/0003/367383/julielogan-dyslexic-entrepreneurs.pdf

99. Britanncia https://britannica.com/biography/Cesar-Ritz

100. Wikipedia https://en.wikipedia.org/wiki/Richard_D%27Oyly_Carte

101. Wikipedia https://en.wikipedia.org/wiki/Charles_Forte,_Baron_Forte

102. Wikipedia https://en.wikipedia.org/wiki/Conrad_Hilton

103. Wikipedia https://en.wikipedia.org/wiki/J._Willard_Marriott

104. Britannica https://britannica.com/biography/Paul-Bocuse

105. Wikipedia https://en.wikipedia.org/wiki/Pierre_Bellon

106. Wikipedia https://en.wikipedia.org/wiki/J._Willard_Marriott

107. Tony Mayo https://tonymayo.com/marriott-happy-employees-happy-customers/

108. "Year to Success." Bo Bennett 2015 https://books.google.co.uk/books?id=xwdUEzMZBP4C&pg=PT554&lpg=PT554&dq=%22My+father+gave+me+the+responsibility+of+a+man,%22+said+Marriott+many+years+later.+%22He+would+tell+me+what+he+wanted+done,+but+never+said+much+about+how+to+do+it.+It+was+up+to+me+to+find+out+for+myself%E2%80%9D&source=bl&ots=KSYwSNo9-l&sig=ACfU3U3fz4XTiQWTSDdvMYAMa3ZtNWNb6Q&hl=en&sa=X&ved=2ahUKEwjng9rnuIPpAhV_ShUIHUqtA4QQ6AEwAXoECAoQAQ#v=onepage&q=%22My%20father%20gave%20me%20the%20responsibility%20of%20a%20man%2C%22%20said%20Marriott%20many%20years%20later.%20%22He%20would%20tell%20me%20what%20he%20wanted%20done%2C%20but%20never%20said%20much%20about%20how%20to%20do%20it.%20It%20was%20up%20to%20me%20to%20find%20out%20for%20myself%E2%80%9D&f=false

109. Quotefancy https://quotefancy.com/quote/1558647/J-Willard-Marriott-A-man-should-keep-on-being-constructive-and-do-constructive-things-He

110. Leadership profile. Conrad Hilton 2014 by Morgan Bailey, Juan Mendez and Jianwu Zhai https://scholarworks.umass.edu/cgi/viewcontent.cgi?article=1017&context=palat

111. Conde Neste Traveller. Laura Fowler https://cntraveller.com/gallery/claridges-hotel-london-uk-review

112. Claridges https://claridges.co.uk/

113. Magnolia Box https://magnoliabox.com/products/mivarts-hotel-brook-street-near-grosvenor-square-westminster-london-1645710

114. Britanncia https://britannica.com/biography/Auguste-Escoffier

115. The Washington Post 4th May 1980 Geoffrey Robinson https://washingtonpost.com/archive/lifestyle/1980/05/04/the-king-of-chefs-and-the-chef-of-kings/081a73b4-1226-4514-8f9e-e340bf139d50/

116. Wikipedia https://en.wikipedia.org/wiki/Rosa_Lewis
117. Wikipedia https://en.wikipedia.org/wiki/The_Duchess_of_Duke_Street
118. The Telegraph 15th December 2005 https://telegraph.co.uk/foodanddrink/
     3323406/We-live-too-long-to-have-just-one-woman.html
119. Quartz. 21st Jan 2018 David Gershgorn https://qz.com/quartzy/1184999/
     paul-bocuses-classic-technique-is-still-important-in-an-era-of-youtube-
     chefs/
120. The Washington Post   21st Jan 2018 https://washingtonpost.com/
     local/obituaries/paul-bocuse-french-chef-who-popularized-nouvelle-
     cuisine-movement-dies-at-91/2018/01/20/d97ce864-fde3-11e7-a46b-
     a3614530bd87_story.html
121. Wikipedia https://en.wikipedia.org/wiki/Ken_McCulloch
122. Mercatus. 10th September 2012 by Cecil Bohanon https://mercatus.org/
     publications/economic-history/economic-recovery-lessons-post-world-
     war-ii-period
123. Mercatis 10th September 2012. By Cecil Bohanon https://mercatus.org/
     publications/economic-history/economic-recovery-lessons-post-world-
     war-ii-period
124. "War and Market Economy" by   Lester B Stone. 1st Feb 2017
     https://books.google.co.uk/books?id=RAY1DgAAQBAJ&pg=PT163&
     lpg=PT163&dq=A+poll+of+business+executives+in+1944+and+1945+
     revealed+that+only+8.5+percent+of+them+thought+the+prospects+for+
     their+company+had+worsened+in+the+post-war+period.&source=
     bl&ots=0218S6C37p&sig=ACfU3U1ND12v9rpx
     Y5AwHzhqyE6KuTFdhA&hl=en&sa=X&ved=2ahUKEwiGia
     yWwIPpAhVgURUIHW5DCYQQ6AEwAHoECAkQAQ#v=o
     nepage&q=A%20poll%20of%20business%20executives%20in%20
     1944%20and%201945%20revealed%20that%20only%208.5%20
     percent%20of%20them%20thought%20the%20prospects%20for%20
     their%20company%20had%20worsened%20in%20the%20post-
     war%20period.&f=false
125. The Genius Works 2nd March 2017 https://thegeniusworks.com/2017/03/
     dream-big-let-passion-shine-richard-bransons-poem-entrepreneurs/
126. Wikipedia https://en.wikipedia.org/wiki/Clive_Woodward

About the Author

Chris Sheppardson is the founder of a leading hospitality consultancy—EP, Business in Hospitality (founded 2005)—which specializes in progressive thinking and in bringing together industry leaders to debate key issues of the day plus publishes regular articles on the major topics. Chris is also the founder of Chess Partnership (founded 1998), which is a leading recruitment concern for senior appointments in hospitality. Chris has had previous books published in the fields of both hospitality and sport—*The Luxury Hotels of London* (1991), *Leadership and Entrepreneurship in the Hospitality Industry* (2011), *If Only* (2015), *For the Love of the Game* (2016).

Researcher: Iwona Drozdz

Iwona joined EP in 2019 and is a trained psychotherapist. Iwona conducted many of the interviews with industry leaders, which are quoted within the body of the text.

Index

OTHER TITLES IN THE TOURISM AND HOSPITALITY MANAGEMENT COLLECTION

Betsy Bender Stringam, New Mexico State University, Editor

- *Cultural and Heritage Tourism and Management* by Tammie J. Kaufman
- *Marine Tourism, Climate Change, and Resilience in the Caribbean, Volume II* by Kreg Ettenger and Samantha Hogenson
- *Marketing Essentials for Independent Lodging* by Pamela Lanier and Marie Lanier
- *Marine Tourism, Climate Change, and Resiliency in the Caribbean, Volume I* by Kreg Ettenger and Samantha Hogenson
- *Catering and Convention Service Survival Guide in Hotels and Casinos* by Lisa Lynn Backus and Patti J. Shock
- *Coastal Tourism, Sustainability, and Climate Change in the Caribbean, Volume II* by Martha Honey and Kreg Ettenger
- *Coastal Tourism, Sustainability, and Climate Change in the Caribbean, Volume I* by Martha Honey and Kreg Ettenger
- *The Good Company* by Robert Girling and Heather Gordy

Announcing the Business Expert Press Digital Library

Concise e-books business students need for classroom and research

This book can also be purchased in an e-book collection by your library as

- a one-time purchase,
- that is owned forever,
- allows for simultaneous readers,
- has no restrictions on printing, and
- can be downloaded as PDFs from within the library community.

Our digital library collections are a great solution to beat the rising cost of textbooks. E-books can be loaded into their course management systems or onto students' e-book readers. The **Business Expert Press** digital libraries are very affordable, with no obligation to buy in future years. For more information, please visit **www.businessexpertpress.com/librarians**. To set up a trial in the United States, please email **sales@businessexpertpress.com**.

www.ingramcontent.com/pod-product-compliance
Lightning Source LLC
Chambersburg PA
CBHW071252220526
45468CB00001B/93